Signs and Wonders

TO SEEK OR NOT TO SEEK

EXPLORING THE POWER OF THE MIRACULOUS
TO BRING PEOPLE TO FAITH IN GOD

BEN R. PETERS

Foreword by
Bill Hamon

Signs and Wonders

© 2002 by Ben Peters

Library of Congress Control Number: 2002114806
ISBN 0-9767685-4-2

Unless otherwise indicated, Bible quotations are taken from the New King James Version. Copyright © 1983 by Thomas Nelson, Inc. Also: Parts of verses highlighted or underlined or in italics are the personally added emphases of the author.

Cover art used by permission of Robert Bartow
www.bartowimages.com

Open Heart Ministries
15648 Bombay Blvd.
S. Beloit, IL 61080
www.ohmint.org
benrpeters@juno.com

Signs and Wonders

Thorough ... biblical ... honest ... sensitive. Ben Peters has done a commendable job in attempting to build a bridge between two streams of Christianity over the sensitive issue of the miraculous. While this effort is not a defense of signs or wonder or an attack against those who do not yet embrace them, it is a call for the evangelical Church to use every tool God has granted Her to bring people into His Kingdom. Ben's biblical and historical research is very compelling and, if his proposal is accepted, should advance evangelism greatly. I highly recommend it.

Paul D. Hunter, Senior Minister
Timber Valley Church, Colton Oregon

Ben Peters' book, *"Signs and Wonders: To Seek or Not To Seek"* is a unique book. I know of no other on this specific subject. It will be a great encouragement to believers who share their faith with the unsaved. Signs and wonders are primarily for the authentication of the gospel and should be taking place far more often in the marketplace than in the sanctuary. I am happy to give my endorsement to the thesis of the book and pray that it will be widely read and even more widely practiced.

Maurice L. Fuller, Former Bible College Professor
and Senior Pastor of Queens Park Full Gospel Church
Calgary, Alberta, Canada

The Bible begins with God's supernatural power being manifested in Creation. The book *Signs and Wonders* shows the same power of the same God being actively demonstrated throughout both the Old and New Testaments. Author Ben Peters clearly weaves a scriptural pattern showing God in action continuing to touch the lives of mankind in supernatural ways.

This is a very balanced presentation which leaves the reader with a deep hunger for a greater measure of God's presence. It also stirs a cry from deep withing, "God, do it again!"

Robert Smith, Senior Pastor
West Calgary Full Gospel Church

My life has been enriched for having known Elmer Burnette and Ben Peters. Whether it is the mentor (Elmer Burnette) or the mentored (Ben Peters) both men have discovered, and have lived by a balanced understanding of love (1 Corinthians 13) and the gifts (1 Corinthians 12 and 14). It is from this balanced and unselfish perspective that this book has been written, so why not read on and receive both the spirit and knowledge of what has been written by Ben Peters.

Arlo A. Johnson, Senior Pastor
Westside Family Fellowship
Prince George, B.C., Canada

Signs and Wonders: To Seek or Not to Seek is like an e-mail from the Father's Heart to the human spirit. God's truths burst forth as instant messages. How high-tech and deep-rooted are His mysteries (Jer. 33:3) in His Love for us. Showers of blessings (Ezek. 34:26) flow forth from these pages. To write "Signs and Wonders" Ben Peters certainly accessed the heavenly website of the glorious "I AM."

Barbara E. Fard, wife and mother
President of Crystal Lake Aglow Lighthouse ,
a local outreach of Aglow International
Crystal Lake, Illinois

"This book is a much needed read for every Christian worker and even the critic who desires to know New Testament Christianity in it's operative fullness. The theology is sound, backed by a well documented view of history and relevant to the present day. I like the spirit that is demonstrated by the author".

Tim Osiowy, Senior Pastor
Gateway Christian Ministries
Prince George, B.C. Canada

My faith was stirred, as I read "Signs and Wonders." This book represents a fresh word to the Body of Christ.

Ben Peters' "Signs and Wonders" comes at the "kairos" or opportune time because now is the most difficult, yet exciting time in the history of the world to be a Christ follower.

We the Church, including Evangelical, Fundamentalist, Pentecostal and Charismatic believers all need to have our faith stirred. Signs and Wonders will bring the lost to Christ. This book brings a fresh, encouraging and strengthening word to us.

Ben Peters' "Signs and Wonders" has the potential to bring true unity to the Church for such a time as this.

Dr. Cheryl Roush Armstrong, Pastor
Fresh Harvest Church, Woodstock, Illinois
and Apostle from Fresh Harvest Ministries.

A thoroughly Biblical presentation on a critical issue.

D. S. Fenn, Senior Pastor
Calgary Full Gospel Church

Contents

Foreword

If you are not fully convinced that signs and wonders are for Christians then you need to read this book with an open heart and mind. Ben R. Peters gives numerous Biblical proofs from the Old and New Testaments. He reveals the meaning of signs and wonders and what they are to accomplish. He follows the principles of Biblical hermeneutics in giving undeniable proof that signs and wonders are to be a definite part of every Christian's life and ministry. Signs and wonders are not given to satisfy curiosity or one's desire to experience and manifest signs and wonders but they are designed to convey a message from God to His creation. Those who believe in signs and wonders need to read this book to build their faith to where they are consistently manifesting God's signs and wonders.

In my latest book called "The Day of the Saints" I prophetically declare that there is a coming saints movement. Those who are properly prepared will manifest God's miraculous signs and wonders. Every saint will be full believers who have all the signs of a believer. The supernatural will have become a way of life to them. God wants demonstrated on earth that there is no God like His Son, Jesus Christ. The saints who are ready to be the full manifestation of the Body of Christ on earth will make the false religions look powerless. They will manifest supernatural prophetic insight, prophesy accurately and powerful like the Elijah Prophet of old. Apostolic signs and wonders will be manifest mightily until all others declare like Nebuchadnezzar did that there is no god like the most High God, which is Jesus Christ, the God of true Christianity. The Kingdom of God must be preached and demonstrated with powerful signs and wonders. The Church today is not demonstrating the lordship of Christ Jesus but they soon will.

This book is a must reading and study guide for those who want to have the revelation and faith to manifest the Kingdom of God with mighty signs and wonders. Read to understand, believe and demonstrate to the world that Jesus Christ is the only true God. We will then reap the great end time harvest that God has ordained for this generation.

Thank you Ben for giving the vital and timely book to prepare the saints for their full day of manifesting God's glory until it fills the earth as the waters cover the sea.

Dr. Bill Hamon
Founder/President
Christian International Ministries Network

Preface

While writing this book, I was impressed in my spirit that I must be careful to present this teaching in such a way that it won't polarize or produce division in the body of Christ. Rather, it is our desire, as well as the Lord's, that in everything we do in ministry, we strive to build and protect the unity of the Spirit, in the bond of peace.

In keeping with this imperative from the Lord, I want to make it clear that we desire to present our research in a kind and humble manner. Though I feel strongly about the subject and the importance of using God's tools and weapons to bring in the harvest and defeat His enemy, I do feel it is very counterproductive to argue my point with the wrong spirit.

Having already written much of the book when I felt this nudging from the Lord, I reread what I had already written, and made several changes to take away any argumentative or adversarial tone. My natural tendency is to aggressively debate and argue my point, especially when I feel strongly that I am right. But I am reminded that in the flesh I can't please God.

Therefore, to those who do not see things eye-to-eye with me, I want to express my hope that what I have written will not be offensive, or in any way insensitive to your own sincere convictions. Rather, I trust that you will feel free to objectively examine the research presented in this book.

Most Christians are aware of some major divisions in the body of Christ. One of these major divisions is between the Evangelical/Fundamentalist camp (which we shall refer to as the E/F camp), and the Pentecostal/Charismatic camp (which we shall refer to as the P/C camp). **I believe that it is very high on God's agenda in these days that the walls that divide these two camps be brought down.**

God has been pursuing this agenda in some very exciting ways. We have seen leaders from both camps reaching out in special ways to the other camp. Walls are indeed coming down, and we applaud every effort made by either camp towards this goal.

I was personally raised in the P/C camp, but I know that our camp has often lacked the grace and humility that we should have demonstrated. We have often displayed an attitude of super-spirituality, frequently offending unnecessarily those from the other camp. We have sometimes been proud of our differences, even when they appeared strange or weird. And our own insecurity has prompted us to strike back at those who didn't understand us.

I also exhort leaders and members from both camps to reexamine some of the details of their doctrines that have been the most divisive. I know that some of the doctrines boldly proclaimed as absolute truth in our own P/C camp do not have the solid biblical proof to justify the dogmatic stand that we have taken. Some of these doctrines, which I believe have been influenced by spiritual pride, have severely wounded many sincere Christians, and actually prevented others from receiving the blessings that we have received.

Whenever we have come across offensively, defensively or indifferently, we have made it very difficult for those in the E/F camp to listen to us. Instead they have been pressured into proving our doctrines and experiences to be wrong. They reacted to our attitudes and in many cases they rejected our beliefs, because our pride spoke louder than the logic of our doctrinal arguments.

But like two married people who are having marriage problems, we need to learn how to listen to each other. A marriage counselor would teach us how to communicate in a non-offensive manner and to listen to the other person with a deeper concern for their feelings as they speak. If both parties do what they are asked to do by their counselor, both will begin to realize that they have been a part of the problem and both of them can help resolve it.

These two camps need to come together and learn to listen with a passion to understand the concerns of the other camp. As Proverbs 13:10 reminds us, contention comes only from pride. It's not so much our doctrines that divide us; it's our pride in those doctrines. It's the basic need to believe that our doctrines are superior to the doctrines of the other camp. Actually, our doctrines are not really that far apart in many areas.

Also, we need to realize that both camps are fulfilling a needed role in the church today. We really do need each other, and God really needs us in both camps to work together. Only when we come together in unity will we see the awesome power of God revealed the way He wants to reveal it. And only then will we be equipped to reap the fields that are already ripe for the harvest. My earlier book, "Heal Your Body, Lord" deals with this subject of unity in much greater detail. Since the writing of that book, I am even more convinced that bringing His children into harmony is a major passion of the Father's heart.

So to those in both camps, please keep your heart and mind open as you examine the research recorded in this book. Let God give you a fervent cry for the salvation of lost souls and for the kind of revival in the church that will produce again a bountiful harvest. Let the church bring in that harvest from every inhabited place on the face of the earth and let us do it all for the sake of the Lord of the harvest.

Dedication

It is my joy to dedicate this book to the memory of Elmer R. Burnette, the man who not only mentored me, along with my wife, Brenda, for more than eight years, but also demonstrated so consistently to us and others, both the love and the power of Jesus. It is also dedicated to the memory of Evelyn Burnette, his first wife, and his daughters, Karen Buchanan and Kathy Villman, who all preceded him to Heaven. It is also dedicated to David Burnette, his son, and Bonnie Dick, his daughter, and finally to his widow, Madeline (Maggie) Burnette, of Albany, Oregon, who walked with him and cared for him during his later years on this earth.

Because of Elmer Burnette's ministry, I was privileged to see the mighty hand of God at work in places like India, Argentina, and Colombia, as well as in Canada and the United States. In Argentina, especially, we were extremely blessed to see the awesome signs and wonders that brought more than one thousand souls to Jesus in six powerful weeks.

Although he was not famous in many Christian circles, this man represented the best of God's faithful servants. A man who dearly loved God, he had little personal ambition to make a name for himself. He never charged for his services, but he was always giving generously from his own limited resources. He wrote four books, started seven or eight churches, raised up a ministry in India with about fifty native pastors and traveled extensively for many years. He was used by God to bring salvation to tens of thousands, both directly, and through those who became evangelists, pastors and missionaries through his ministry. He also was used to bring divine healing to many thousands more in over forty years of faithful service.

Elmer has been enjoying Heaven for several years now, but the spiritual seeds he sowed on this planet during his lifetime are still bearing beautiful fruit and will continue to do so until the Lord of the Harvest comes to receive it to Himself.

CHAPTER 1

Tackling the Tough Question

A LIFE-IMPACTING PERSONAL EXPERIENCE

The middle-aged couple listened with interest to the preaching of my mentor, Elmer Burnette, as he shared the living gospel with the small crowd which had gathered that evening. The couple owned the hotel that was hosting our meetings in the city of La Falda, Argentina. They had been curious about this group of Protestants who had rented their hall week after week. Several times before, out of curiosity, they had sat in the back of the hall, as they were doing this very night.

But this night was to be a very unique and life-changing experience for them both. After sharing from the Bible, Brother Burnette (as everyone called him) started praying for the sick. Then he motioned to the couple to come forward, as he felt God wanted to touch them. As he began to pray for the wife, she began to open and close her hands, and tears began streaming down her face. Then her husband saw what was happening and tears began streaming down his face as well.

We discovered that she had been suffering from severe and painfully crippling arthritis, and had not been able to even open her hands for some time. The miracle took place in a moment and they were both weeping profusely.

Brother Burnette asked them if they wanted to accept the same Jesus, who had healed them, as their Savior and Lord. They both immediately responded in the affirmative through their tears and sobs of joy. They received a healing in one moment and salvation in the next.

That was just one of many examples of the power of the miraculous to facilitate faith in someone that was previously an unbeliever. We saw over one thousand other examples in those glorious six weeks in Argentina in the fall of 1973. Every meeting in those six weeks was an awesome display of God's supernatural power. Following many amazing words of knowledge and miracles of healing, the altar was opened to those who wanted Jesus, this powerful Healer, to be their personal Savior. And every night many would come with tears streaming down their faces to receive Jesus.

Lest anyone think that these decisions were simply emotional and temporary, we were told one year later that five new churches had sprung up in the various places where these meetings had occurred, and only one church had less than 200 people. That was a great encouragement to us that the majority of the new converts had been established in the Kingdom of God.

A PASTOR DISCOVERS A POWERFUL EVANGELISTIC TOOL

A young pastor of the mid-twentieth century heard a call from God to focus on a healing ministry. He rented an auditorium and asked God for a crowd of 1000, which was about seven times the size of his own congregation. Over 1,200 showed up. He prayed for the sick, and suddenly a woman who had a stiff and paralyzed hand began shouting and waving her totally-healed hand.

Very soon he felt a tugging from behind him and turned around. There, standing before him, were seven men, who were the unbelieving husbands of women who attended his church. They had all been very antagonistic towards their wives regarding his church, and now, because of what they had seen, they were asking for forgiveness and wanted to be saved. The young preacher's name was Oral Roberts.

STRIPPER FINDS JESUS AS HEALER/SAVIOR

Our daughter recently heard a testimony of one of her Bible College classmates. The beautiful young woman told her story in the third person, only revealing herself as the subject of the story when the story was done. She had suffered a terribly abusive childhood, and was exposed to drugs and immorality from her earliest memory.

Her young adult lifestyle ultimately led her to become a stripper. Finally, she became very ill, and in desperation, she called a Christian aunt for prayer. When the aunt prayed for her, she was instantly healed. When her aunt invited her to church she accepted, and in the service, she boldly responded to the salvation invitation.

Her life was so transformed, and she was such a radiant Christian, that everyone who heard her story was totally stunned. The student body was impacted with the truth that miracles have the power to get someone's attention and convince them of the reality of God's love.

WHERE DO WE GO WITH THIS?

Stories like these abound in contemporary Christianity around the globe. People are still responding with decisive faith in God when they see God perform miracles before their eyes. And yet today, many Christian leaders continue to reject or put down those who put any focus on signs and wonders.

Many still proclaim the theory that all miracles ceased after the death of the first twelve apostles. Others believe in miracles, but have had little success in producing them and have resigned themselves to bringing people to faith through the more natural methods of evangelism rather than through supernatural signs and wonders.

Now we want to make it clear that we understand that some of the opposition to the supernatural is not really opposition to the power of God, but rather to the methods and personalities of the people who proclaim the supernatural. We know that it is very easy to offend others with a sense of spiritual superiority and many have been turned off to this whole aspect of Christianity, because of the spirit of the messenger.

But we would ask the reader to lay aside personal feelings or presuppositions that have come from their own life experiences, and make an effort to listen with an open mind and heart to the voice of the Holy Spirit. **Please come with me as we embark on a great adventure into the biblical record and ask this question –** *When people became believers in the Bible, what were the factors that brought them to faith?*

In addition to our biblical study we will also take a very brief look at some post-biblical church history to examine the different ways that people are being brought to faith. We will discover the impact that the miraculous has had and is still having in bringing people to faith in God and especially in Jesus Christ as Lord and Savior. If our time on earth is limited, (and we know it is) then we want to bring as many people to faith as possible.

The question is: *"What is the most efficient use of our time and energy, with regards to bringing people to faith in God? Has God actually given us a recipe or a pattern to produce powerful "Faith-Makers", or are we left with only the same natural means of persuasion as a good salesman would use to sell a good product?"*

THE ANTI-SIGN PROOF TEXT

Jesus declared, "Unless you *people* see signs and wonders you will by no means believe." (John 4:48)

He also said, "An evil and adulterous generation seeks after a sign, and no sign shall be given it except the sign of the prophet Jonah" (Matthew 12:39). Many Bible teachers and even song writers have made bold negative statements about Christians who seek after signs, wonders and miracles, based primarily on the latter verse.

One day, while helping my wife with some laundry in an El Cajon, California, Laundromat, a man began passing out tracts and talking to the patrons. He was boldly proclaiming that people who sought after miracles were false teachers, and those who believed because of miracles were not true believers and probably not really saved. He quoted Jesus' words in the above Matthew 12 passage as a proof-text.

18

I began to share a few other Scriptures with him and tried to get him to take a more biblical perspective on this teaching, but he couldn't open his mind to anything that would derail his anti-miracle express. The next time we saw him at the Laundromat, he carefully avoided any conversation with us.

On another occasion, I heard on Christian radio a popular radio preacher making some incredible statements. He declared that people who kept seeking after signs and wonders were just not willing to abide by God's rules. God was not doing miracles any more and we needed to accept that. In fact, if anyone reported an actual miracle taking place, we know that it was of the devil, because the devil was the only one doing miracles today. I had a hard time believing that any Christian Bible teacher could say what he was saying. And I found it equally difficult to believe that others could concur with his point of view.

OUR GOALS FOR THIS BOOK

In this book, we will reexamine the purpose for signs, wonders and miracles, and what our position or attitude should be towards these biblical phenomena. We will discover some amazing biblical facts, and come to a greater understanding of God's awesome ways. We will attempt to understand why Jesus made the interesting statements quoted above and how they fit in with the rest of His revolutionary teachings and practices.

Above all, I pray that all readers will clearly hear in their hearts the passionate cry of the "Lord of the Harvest", pleading with us to use all the awesome, incredible tools, as well as the natural talents, that He has given us in order to fulfill the "Great Commission". May we with great desire pursue Him and the explosive expansion of His great Kingdom, without neglecting the blessed "vehicle of miracle", which He has entrusted to us.

THE CASE FOR SEEKING SIGNS AND WONDERS

Remembering that Scripture must be compared with the whole body of Scripture before we draw theological conclusions, let's begin a preliminary investigation of biblical references to signs and wonders.

First of all, let's take another look at the two verses quoted above. We need to realize what these statements do **not** say.

The first statement made by Jesus (John 4:48) was to the noble-man (or royal official) whose son was sick and dying in Capernaum. Jesus said, *"Unless you see signs and wonders, you will by no means believe."* This is not necessarily a negative or critical statement. **It may be just a very significant statement of fact.**

Jesus may indeed have been expressing some disappointment that people wouldn't believe without a sign or wonder, but **He knew that if He didn't show the miraculous power of God, people would not believe in Him and they would not be saved.** Oh how great it would be if most people would believe without a supernatural revelation of the power and majesty of God, but **Jesus made it clear that many would not believe without the supernatural.**

Jesus responded to the nobleman's plea for help and said, "Go your way; your son lives." The next statement in the same verse is: "So the man **believed** the word that Jesus spoke to him, and he went his way" (John 4:50). The next three verses explain how the son was healed at the same hour as Jesus said, "Your son lives."

Then at the end of verse 53 we read, **"And he himself believed, and his whole household."** Verse 54 tells us that this was the second "sign" that Jesus did in Galilee. So we must ask the obvious questions.

1. Was Jesus critical of the people or not?
2. If he was, why did he do the sign?
3. Did people believe because of the sign?

The answer to the last question is obviously, YES! For the answer to the first two, let the reader be the judge. Hopefully, we will be able to help the reader form more accurate conclusions as we proceed.

The second, and the most commonly quoted verse, (Matthew

12:39) is a little tougher to deal with, but let us tackle it now. Jesus said to the scribes and Pharisees, *"An evil and adulterous generation seeks after a sign, and no sign will be given to it except the sign of the prophet Jonah."* The sign of the prophet Jonah was a prophetic sign that He (Jesus) would be in the heart of the earth three days and nights, as Jonah was in the belly of the whale.

First of all, let's look at the basic logic of those who use this verse to judge those who seek God for signs and wonders in our contemporary church life. What they (and the zealous man in the Laundromat) are assuming is that Jesus was saying that **everyone** who seeks signs is evil or adulterous. In Logic 101, we called that kind of thinking *"reasoning from the many to the all".*

To illustrate, let's make another statement. "Wicked people are waiting for darkness." The reason would be so that they can commit crimes unnoticed. Now, if I am also waiting for darkness so I can light off my legal fireworks on the Fourth of July, does that make me a wicked person? Of course not! But that is exactly the logic we are applying if we imply that anyone and everyone seeking a sign is part of an "evil and adulterous generation."

TRY THIS ON FOR SIZE

Consider this possibility. Let's hypothesize that seeking after signs **with good motives**, is a good thing that good people do. (We trust you will see the clear biblical evidence in this book to back up this hypothesis.) Along comes a group of deceitfully wicked people, hypocritically pretending to be sincerely seeking after a sign with good motives (a good thing to do). Jesus responds, "You wicked and adulterous generation, are you actually faking sincerity in your seeking a sign? I know your deception and hypocrisy. You are nothing but phony hypocrites and so I will give you no sign except one which you won't understand."

This may be just a hypothesis, but I believe you will see it as the most reasonable interpretation of this verse, based on the rest of the Scripture, which relates to this subject. As we shall see, there were times that God actually instructed or even commanded people to ask for a sign, because He desired to reveal His glory and build the faith of the people.

By the way, what did Jesus mean when He used the word "adulterous"? I believe He meant that they were not faithful to the public vows they had made to God. They were officially married to God, but were more in love with the god of power and popularity than they were with their Creator.

They acted like they wanted to see God reveal His power so they could honor Him and worship Him. This story is similar to that of King Herod who told the wise men that He wanted to find out where little baby Jesus was so He could also worship Him. But Herod had other motives, and so did the Pharisees. They wanted Him to do something that they could find fault with so that they could tell everyone that He was a fake.

In other words, Jesus knew their scheme to discredit him and wouldn't play their little game. They were not interested in truth, but rather in discrediting anyone who was a threat to their position of power and prestige.

Later on a gathering of the same religious leaders made the self-incriminating statement:

> "What shall we do to these men? For indeed, that *a notable miracle has been done* through them is evident to all who dwell in Jerusalem, and *we cannot deny it.*" Acts 4:16

And thus Jesus knew that a sign would be totally useless to change their hearts. And that was where their problem resided; in their hearts, not in their minds.

But to those who had sincere and hungry hearts, Jesus would show an incredible array of miraculous signs and wonders. Later He would declare that they should believe in the works (miracles) that He did, if they had trouble believing who He was (John 10:38). In other words, "Let the miracles done before your eyes be 'signs' that show you that I truly am the Son of God."

JOHN SEEKS CONFIRMATION

When the incarcerated John the Baptist sent two of his disciples to Jesus to ask if He was really the Messiah, Jesus responded by doing many signs and miracles that very hour. Then He told John's disciples to report on the things that they had seen (Luke 7:18-23). These signs were done for John the Baptist because he was a sincere inquirer, not a deceiver like the wicked scribes and Pharisees.

GOD COMMANDS A KING TO ASK FOR A SIGN

We also have an Old Testament record where **God actually told a king to ask for a sign** (Isaiah 7:10-14). When King Ahaz refused, he was rebuked by God and was given a sign from God, even though he declined to ask for one. This record indicates that **an evil and adulterous generation does not always seek for a sign**. King Ahaz was certainly evil and adulterous and yet he refused to ask for a sign. He was rebuked by God for it, and then given a sign, even though he hadn't asked for one.

APOSTLES CRY OUT FOR SIGNS AND WONDERS

There is one more essential story that merits close attention at this point. In the book of Acts, we find the powerful Jerusalem church under serious persecution. This persecution took place concurrent with a multitude of signs and wonders, which began to attract followers by the thousands. In Acts, chapter four, after being threatened by the Sanhedrin, the apostles came back to their companions and reported the results of their hearing.

They all immediately went to prayer, asking God to give them boldness to disobey the command of the religious leaders of their nation. Now please read carefully the apostles' prayer in the following verses.

"Now Lord, look on their threats, and grant to Your servants that with all boldness they may speak your word, by stretching forth your hand to heal, and **that signs and wonders may be done through the name of Your holy Servant Jesus**." And when they had prayed, the place where they were assembled together was shaken; and they were all filled with the Holy Spirit, and they spoke the word of God with boldness. (Luke 4: 29-31)

Did you notice what they prayed for? Yes, they prayed for boldness to speak for God. But how did they want that boldness to come? Was it through strength of character? Was it through wise strategy? Both would have been good things to pray for, but they prayed for something else instead. **They prayed first for healings, and second for signs and wonders to energize their courage.**

Obviously these early apostles were not a part of the "wicked and adulterous generation" that Jesus spoke to earlier on. Why would these apostles of the Lamb seek after healings, signs and wonders, if that would identify them with a wicked and adulterous generation? With all sincere respect to those who have entertained a different point of view, I think this story should deal a final and fatal blow to the belief that it's wrong to ask God for signs and wonders. We must conclude that **asking or seeking for signs and wonders can be either good or bad, depending on the motives of the heart.**

WHAT ABOUT THE CESSATIONIST VIEW?

Some will use the argument, based on an interpretation of I Corinthians 13:8-13, that spiritual gifts have all passed away, and we are living in a different dispensation than the early church. But I believe that this interpretation has no validity for several reasons.

The first reason is that Jesus made the statement about an evil and adulterous generation to the Pharisees in His own time or dispensation, not in ours. So clearly, His rebuke for seeking signs and wonders had nothing to do with the passing into a new dispensation. His rebuke came in the same time period as the one in which He performed almost every imaginable sign and wonder for the common people. Therefore, there can be no connection with this verse and the I Corinthians passage.

Also, the context of I Corinthians 13:10 makes it clear that the gifts won't pass away until Jesus returns. "That which is perfect" is not referring to the Bible being completed, but rather it refers to Jesus return, when "we will see him face to face" and "know Him even as we are known". And there is no portion of Scripture anywhere in the Bible that prophesies the cessation of the Holy Spirit's gifts, or of signs and wonders until that day.

In fact, Joel prophesies that in the last days God would pour out His Spirit on all flesh with prophetic gifts and signs and wonders. If Pentecost was the beginning of the last days, we are definitely still in the last days, and indeed we are seeing God pour out His Spirit and His gifts upon the body of Jesus, His dear Son.

Some Bible teachers have taught the following explanation for this "last days" concept. One day is as one thousand years to God (II Peter 3:8). About 4,000 years (four millenniums) had passed since Adam when Jesus came to earth, and the church began at the beginning of the fifth millennium or the fifth "day". If God's dealing with man on earth is a seven "day" week, then the fourth "day" would be the middle day, and the fifth day would be the beginning of the last three days.

First Three Days	Middle Day	Last Three Days
Day 1 Day 2 Day 3	Day 4	Day 5 Day 6 Day 7

With the seventh day (or Sabbath) attributed to the millennium reign of Jesus on the earth, the sixth day, which has just past (by our calendar), would be the last of the last days before Jesus' return, from this particular interpretation of eschatology. Thus Pentecost happened early in Day 5, which was the first of the last three days. We are now at the beginning of the last of the last days, according to our western calendar.

Whether you accept this interpretation or not, it should still be safe to conclude that we are still in the days that Joel prophesied, "And it shall come to pass in the last days . . ." There is another, and probably more powerful argument for the conviction that we are still in the same period known as the last days. It is the fact that Joel's prophecy continues, and is quoted by Peter to state that during these last days, "whoever calls on the name of the Lord shall be saved." (Joel 2:32, Acts 2:21). Pentecost was the beginning of that time period and we are still in that same Kingdom age.

GOD ANSWERS THE APOSTLES' PRAYER FOR SIGNS AND WONDERS

After the apostles' prayer for boldness, the first thing that happened was that the place was shaken. The shaking was a "sign." It was a sign that God had heard and was making His powerful presence felt, confirming that He planned to answer their prayers.

Then we read that they were all filled with the Holy Spirit. We can only speculate on what actually happened when this event took place, but based on other similar instances, there was presumably some clear and obvious supernatural manifestation of the Holy Spirit. Immediately after this the Scripture says, ". . . they spoke the word of God with boldness."

In the following few verses in Acts 4, we read about great unity and sacrificial dedication, as well as the fact that the apostles boldly gave witness to the resurrection of Jesus "with great power." Great power implies to me (based on the context in Acts) that God showed his power through signs and wonders in a demonstration that Jesus was truly alive.

Following this event in Acts 4 we read on into Acts 5, which over-flows with a variety of references to the supernatural power of God. First we have two powerful prophetic words of knowledge, followed by the apostolic administration of divine justice on Ananias and Sapphira. In verse twelve, after this event, we read that "through the hands of the apostles, many *signs and wonders* were done among the people."

Right after this story we read of **possibly the greatest healing event in the history of the Christian church to this time**. We read that the people of Jerusalem brought the sick into the streets, in the hope that the shadow of Peter would pass over them. Verse sixteen adds,

"Also a multitude gathered from the surrounding cities to Jerusa-
lem, bringing sick people and those who were tormented by unclean
spirits, and they were all healed."

Here we have multitudes of people from both Jerusalem and all
the surrounding cities bringing their sick and demented folks and
lining them up at the side of the street. The most significant differen-
tiating detail of this crusade from most contemporary ones is that,
"They were all healed."

My personal guess is that there were thousands of people healed
as Peter walked by. This assumption is based on the fact that medical
knowledge was very limited and there were no cures for most diseases.
But the most significant fact is not the number of people healed,
but the number of those who were not healed – zero. According
to Luke, the beloved physician, who wrote the book of Acts, **not one**
sick or demented person returned home with the affliction with
which they came.

Luke did not even say that only those whom Peter's shadow
touched were healed. He said that the people were placed in the
street, hoping the shadow of Peter might fall on some of them. But
he boldly declares that they were all healed, whether Peter's shadow
actually touched them or not.

Let us again ask the important question. Did God answer the
disciples' prayer for healings, signs and wonders, for which they
prayed back in chapter four? Or did He rebuke them and call them
a wicked and adulterous bunch of hypocrites for asking for a sign?

It should be crystal clear that God was not upset with the apostles.
Rather, He was obviously thrilled with their request, because it came
from hearts that were infected with the passions of His own heart.
Their only motivation was to prosper His Kingdom, not their own,
and their hearts were not wicked and adulterous, like the hearts of
the scribes and Pharisees.

CHAPTER 2

Belief and Its Relationship to Signs, Wonders and Miracles

In order to understand the purpose of signs, wonders and miracles, we need to take a quick look at the whole concept of "faith" or "belief". Though some Bible teachers have tried to distinguish between faith and belief, there is absolutely no biblical or rational basis for this idea.

These two English words come from the very same Greek word "pistis". This word implies a **proactive,** rather than a passive response to the person they believe in.

Years ago in seminary, I wrote my master's thesis on the subject of faith, and demonstrated that faith in God is not an unknowable, mystical entity. Faith in God is basically the same commodity as the kind of faith that we place in other human beings.

FAITH ON THE HUMAN OR NATURAL LEVEL

The normal basis of our faith in someone on the human level (aside from the gift of spiritual discernment) is the accumulation of information about them that comes to us through our physical senses. Basically our information about them comes through what we observe them doing and what we hear about them from their own mouth and the mouths of others.

In other words, the more that is revealed to us about them, the more we will tend to believe in them, providing that what is revealed about them confirms that they are trustworthy. The more positive information we have about them, the stronger our faith in them will be.

For instance, how many people would you trust out of your sight with your car keys and credit cards, etc. Normally, only those you know and trust from significant experience would be trusted with those important possessions

FAITH IN GOD

The very same principle is at work with our faith in God. But there is a difference, as we all know. We can observe people with our physical senses, but God is a spirit and we cannot see or hear Him the way we can with physical people.

So how can we have faith in God, whom we have not seen? Please don't miss the simple truth we are about to share! **We all, as spiritual beings, have another set of senses,** which I and others call **"spiritual senses".** We see Jesus with spiritual eyes. We hear His voice with spiritual ears. We reach out and touch Him with a spiritual sense of touch; we taste and see that the Lord is good; and we can, at times, sense the fragrance of His presence.

The writer of Hebrews referred to these spiritual senses when he said, "But we see Jesus" (Hebrews 2:9), and "Looking unto Jesus, the author and finisher of our faith" (Hebrews 12:2). Of course, when he said these things, Jesus had taken His place in Heaven and was not visible to human eyes. Paul declared, "Faith comes by hearing and hearing by the word (rhema) of God." These quotes reveal that we have spiritual senses, through which God reveals Himself to us so that we can perceive Him and believe in Him.

NO REVELATION = NO FAITH

This process, of course, is a function of the person of the Holy Spirit who speaks to us in our heart or our spirit and reveals Jesus to us, so that we can believe in Him. Remember that without a person revealing himself to us, we cannot know him and we cannot believe in him. Or put it this way:

No revelation of the person = No faith in the person!

But unbelievers do not have their spiritual senses activated in the same way as Christians, and most Christians don't have their spiritual senses tuned in to God the way they should. How does God reveal Himself to these people?

The answer is simple. **God performs signs and wonders, healings and miracles, that can be seen with the natural eye or heard with the natural ears, so that those who want to know the truth can discover something about God through their natural physical senses. That is what Jesus did in His physical body, and also through the early church, which was His new body on the earth, after His ascension.**

As we will see throughout Scripture, God repeatedly used signs and wonders to make Himself known in order that people would believe in Him. The manifestation of the Holy Spirit in spiritual gifts itself is for the purpose of revealing the presence of Jesus. He has always had a passion to dwell among us, and gave us spiritual gifts specifically for that purpose. (Psalm 68:18)

God's heart is for intimacy and fellowship with His most glorious creation – people like you and me. He has gone to great lengths at much personal cost to restore what He lost in the Garden of Eden. We lost our Paradise and His presence, but He lost the fellowship and intimacy for which He had created us. But through the living body of Jesus on the earth, He continues to seek to make His presence know to all of His creation.

SIGNS

A sign is something set before us to give us information or direction. God has used a multitude of signs throughout history to inform His people. The word "sign" is used 129 times in the King James Version. The Hebrew word means something that appears before us or something that signals a coming event or situation. The Greek word also means something that "signifies". As we will see shortly, there are many other times this word is used, but it is translated as "miracle" many times, instead of "sign".

In Exodus 4:1-9, God gives Moses three signs for the express purpose of causing the Children of Israel to believe that He would deliver them. In verse 8, God declares, "Then it will be, if they do not believe you, nor heed *the message of the first sign*, that they may believe *the message of the latter sign."*

In other words, **the sign had a message.** Signs were not given to entertain, nor were they given to prove the power of the prophet, as the scribes and Pharisees had tried to entice Jesus to do. Rather **signs are given when God has something to communicate with certain people or nations.**

God gave the rainbow as one of His first signs, with the message that He would never again destroy the earth with a flood. Jesus declared in Matthew 24 that there would be signs in the Heaven, with the message that He was coming back soon.

Every sign, by the definition of the word, must have a message! Jesus and the early church performed many signs before the people. And each sign spoke a clear message to the people. Mark declared:

*"These **signs** shall follow them that believe." (Mark: 16:17)*

Mark concludes his gospel with these words:

*"And they went out and preached everywhere, the Lord working with them and confirming the word through the accompanying **signs**. Amen."*

The signs had the message that the word preached was truly of God. The psalmist, Asaph, laments the lack of signs (or messages from God).

*"We do not see our **signs**; There is no longer any prophet; Nor is there any among us who knows how long." (Psalm 74:9)*

When there are no signs from God, it is a time of spiritual famine and a time to cry out passionately to the Lord as Asaph

did, until the Lord begins again to powerfully speak His message in the signs that He performs. (Readers are encouraged to study all of Psalm 74 for the context.)

WONDERS

The definition of a "wonder" is simple. It is a type of supernatural occurrence that is given for the purpose of causing people to wonder what is happening. A wonder causes people to pause from their activities and take notice and meditate or get inspired with what they have seen or heard.

Both of the main Hebrew words which are translated "wonders" imply something unusual or different than the normal. It can also mean something conspicuous that stands out and gets your attention. The New Testament Greek word for "wonder" means "prodigy or omen", speaking of something that indicates a great, or a hidden or mysterious item that has some special meaning or prophetic message. In other words, it makes people ask, "What is the meaning behind this amazing wonder?"

Of the 70 times the word "wonder" is used in the King James Version, it is coupled with the word "signs" (as in "mighty signs and wonders") at least 24 times. This marriage of the two terms indicates that God is most definitely trying to communicate with His people by setting before them something that captures their attention. **It causes them to stand in awe and then speaks an impacting message to them.**

As we will clearly see, God does have His way of impacting people and nations with His signs and wonders. The most emphasized illustration in Scripture is that of the miracles and plagues God did in Egypt, which are called wonders at least 12 times. Before Israel arrived in the promised land, all the nations in the region had heard about the amazing things that God had done in Egypt.

After all, Egypt was the most powerful nation on the earth. And yet the God who was worshipped by a bunch of Hebrew slaves had performed so many awesome miracles that He had totally destroyed the land and all the army of Egypt. From the bloodied waters of the Nile River, to the death of every firstborn child; from the parting of the Red Sea, and the destruction of Egypt's army, to the provision of manna in the wilderness – this amazing story was carried from city to city, and nation to nation, until all the nations in the known world were buzzing with nervous amazement and terrified panic because of the Israelites.

These were the signs and wonders that caught everyone's attention and let them know that the God of Israel was an awesome God. **God's plan for these signs and wonders was first that His people would have a strong faith in Him, and second that they would also encourage other nations to worship their God.**

MIRACLES

The word "miracles" is used only five times in the Old Testament (KJV), but is used 32 times in the New Testament. In both testaments it comes from words that are usually translated "sign". But eight of the 32 New Testament uses of the word "miracle" come from the Greek word, "dunamis" or dynamic power.

Most of these 12 uses refer to the gift of miracles, including the reference in the listing of gifts in I Corinthians 12:10. The working of miracles could really be translated, the working of dynamic power.

We normally think of miracles as events which break the normal laws of nature. Jesus showed His power over natural laws in a multitude of ways. Laws of chemistry were broken when He turned water into wine. The law of gravity was broken when He walked on water. The laws of physics were broken when He multiplied the loaves and fishes. He also revealed His power over sickness, death and demons.

But the truth of the matter is that the Bible does not use any word for miracles that indicates a breaking of natural laws. The two main words used, as mentioned above, indicate an act that provides either a message (in a sign) or a demonstration of dynamic power.

So let's review for a moment. God is trying to get the attention of His creation and produce faith in their hearts so that they can be restored to fellowship with Him. We were not the only ones who lost

34

something in Eden. God also lost intimacy with His own creation. Now, since the fall of man in Eden, He cannot have fellowship with His creation unless He first reveals Himself to them in some supernatural way.

For all those who are truth seekers, but don't have strong spiritual senses, God has ordained that supernatural signs and wonders, and acts of His power should reveal Himself and speak a message to them. Remember that God knows our weaknesses, and His mercy and grace are truly amazing.

It is true that believers, who are walking in intimacy with God, don't have as great a need to see signs for their personal faith as those with weaker spiritual senses. **But like the apostles in Acts 4, we should all desire to see signs and wonders for the sake of His Kingdom.** They, who were already strong in the Holy Spirit, prayed for supernatural manifestations to give them even greater boldness, so that needy men and women would see a revelation of Jesus and put their faith in Him.

THE SCOPE OF THIS STIDY

Before we dig in much deeper to discover the treasures of Scripture, we should explain what we will be looking for. We will not examine every sign or wonder performed by God in the Word. That would require a book too long for me to write and too long for you to read. **We will rather be focusing on every occasion where it was clear that people came to faith in God. We will then be examining what was involved in bringing them to faith.**

We will not only be noting the influence of physical signs and wonders. We will also note the fulfillment of prophetic words, the release of words of knowledge or wisdom, angelic visitations and other revelations. These will include direct divine communication, such as God had with Noah, Abraham and Moses, to name a few.

What we want to compare are the times that people believed as a result of a supernatural revelation, as opposed to the times people believed without any supernatural revelation of God.

Basically, it amounts to this:

1. How frequently did people believe through persuasive speech or other means, without any accompanying supernatural signs and wonders?

2. How frequently did people believe as a result of accompanying signs and wonders that confirmed the spoken word?

We obviously already have a strongly held opinion as we approach this study. But as we try to convince the reader of our beliefs, we will at the same time strive to be objective and come to the conclusions that the facts would lead us to. We will earnestly seek to discover all the scriptural data on both sides of the signs and wonders argument and be totally honest with that data.

Let us begin with a **preliminary thesis**. People are not all alike in what motivates them to believe. Some may be so intellectual that pure logic may convince them. Others may respond to a combination of reason and a strong preaching anointing. Others may not come to a position of faith unless they see a stronger form of proof, such as signs, wonders and miracles.

It is God's desire that all should believe in Him. He knows what it takes, and goes the extra mile to help each sincere individual to believe. He knows how we have been hurt and what it might take to overcome our doubts and inhibitions.

From Genesis through Revelation the Bible reveals that people were moved to faith when they saw signs and wonders. In Genesis, Pharaoh became a believer in God when Joseph interpreted his dream, and in Revelation we are told that because of the signs and wonders performed by the anti-Christ, many will believe in him and he would come close to deceiving even the very elect of God.

In our own ministry experience, we have seen people come to Jesus because of signs and wonders. Many have come to Jesus through a simple prophetic message from God. We have had the privilege of seeing several of these baptized months later, as a testimony to the impact of God's powerful word.

But aside from our own experience, we will demonstrate that the record of the Bible reveals that only a tiny minority of those brought to faith in God came without some demonstration of the supernatural power of God.

Some of these biblical stories show single individuals coming to faith and others show entire nations bowing their knees before the Lord. The more I study these stories, the more convinced I become that signs and wonders were the normal and the usual, rather than the abnormal and unusual means of bringing people to faith in God.

CHAPTER 3

Coming to Faith: The Pre-Mosaic Biblical Record

ADAM THROUGH NOAH

At the beginning of the Genesis account, God was in constant communication with man. It didn't take much for Adam and Eve to believe in God, because He was a personal friend of theirs. As stated earlier, we believe in someone when they reveal themselves to us and we learn that they are trustworthy.

But because of their yielding to the temptation of Satan, which appealed to their pride, Adam and Eve lost that intimacy with God. However, they still had their memories of God and the reality of His Divine presence among them.

Adam lived 930 years. He could tell his descendants about God to the eighth generation. The father of Noah was Lamech, who was born when Adam was 884 years old. Lamech was 46 years old when Adam died.

Therefore, Noah's generation was the first generation that could not have heard a first-hand witness from Adam about what God was like. We do know that God did communicate with people during this time, but we do not know how much or how visibly He appeared to them.

We do know that God talked to Cain, after the murder of Able, and that several generations later, one of Cain's descendants referred to what God had told Cain (Genesis 4:23,24). Thus we know that the stories from the past were still being passed down from generation to generation.

We are also told that after the birth of Enosh, the son of Seth, and the grandson of Adam and Eve, that men began to call upon the name of the Lord (Genesis 4:26). Later, we have the story of Enoch, who was born when Adam was 632 years old and never died, because he walked so close to God that God took him home.

The point we are trying to make with all this information is that there was a significant revelation of God during the pre-Noahic period. People who believed in God during this time had a significant opportunity for direct information about God from Adam and Eve or Cain or Seth.

NOAH'S FAITH COMES BY HEARING

But when Noah came on the scene, Adam had died. Those who walked on the earth had lost the opportunity to talk to anyone who had walked with God in the Garden of Eden. We don't know when Eve died, but I believe it had to be before Noah was born, which was at least1066 years after Adam and Eve's creation. The first 1000-year "day" of man's history was over, and God had said that in the "day" they ate the forbidden fruit, they would surely die.

The new generation needed a fresh revelation of God. But they had fallen prey to the desires of their own flesh and rejected the word that came to them through Noah, a "preacher of righteousness" (II Peter 2:5). The commitment he showed for one hundred years in building the ark, not to mention the very presence of the ark itself, should have been enough of a sign and wonder for them to believe what God was saying through Noah. But they were like the Pharisees, who were not seeking truth, but rather they were seeking for excuses to disbelieve what he had to say.

Therefore, God gave them no other sign. Knowing their hearts, He went on with His plan to destroy them all with the flood.

But Noah was different. God saw Noah's heart and Noah found

grace in the eyes of the Lord (Genesis 6:8). Noah had a heart for God and God gave him a revelation of Himself, speaking to him clearly, giving him directions for the ark. **Faith came by hearing, and hearing came through the direct word of God.**

Even before Noah was given the directions to build the ark, we read that Noah was perfect or blameless in all his ways and that Noah walked with God (Genesis 6:9). Thus we know that God had revealed Himself to Noah repeatedly, because walking with God clearly implies talking with God like the old familiar hymn "In the Garden" relates, "And He walks with me and He talks with me."

THE SIGN OF THE RAINBOW

The first actual use of the word "sign" in the NKJV is found in the story of the first rainbow after the flood. The older KJV uses the word "token", which is used 10 times in the Old Testament in the KJV, but it is the same Hebrew word "sign" which we have already discussed above.

What was the "message of the sign" of the rainbow? The message was that God would not destroy the earth again with a flood. The purpose of the sign was to make the people believe the message, and trust in God's mercy and love.

ABRAHAM BELIEVES GOD AND IS CALLED THE FRIEND OF GOD

The next story involving faith in God is the story of Abraham. Again, we see Abraham responding to a clear revelation of God as He speaks to him and gives him directions to go to another land. Abraham also walked with God in constant communication with Him. I noted over fifty times where Scripture records that God spoke to Abraham, or Abraham spoke with God, or built an altar to worship Him.

Clearly, with Abraham, God was willing to reveal Himself and build his faith in Him. He proved his faith over and over, until God gave him the ultimate test. Since he was already so familiar with the voice of God, there was no doubt in his mind what he had to do. Taking his son, Isaac, up the mountain, he prepared to offer him to God as a sacrifice.

Of course, God intervened at the last moment and spared Isaac.

Abraham was famous for his faith, and he was also called "the friend of God" (James 2:23). Those two descriptions are definitely interrelated. A true friend reveals his heart and soul to us, and we know that we can trust him. It's interesting to note the many ways God revealed Himself to Abraham.

*"Now **the Lord had said** to Abram:" (Genesis 12:1)*

*"Then **the Lord appeared** to Abram and said," (Genesis 12:7)*

*"And **the Lord said** to Abram," (Genesis 13:14)*

"The word of the Lord came to Abram **in a vision."** *(Genesis 15:1)*

There are many more references that repeat the above type of introduction to the communication God had with Abraham. I believe that we too would benefit by asking God for fresh revelation of Himself, so that our faith would grow like the faith of Abraham.

ABRAHAM'S SERVANT ASKS GOD FOR A SIGN

When Abraham's servant was sent to find a wife for Isaac in Genesis 24, **he asked God for a sign** to let him know which woman was to be Isaac's bride. God responded graciously to this request and granted it. He did not rebuke him or deny his request. Because of the convincing "message of the sign" Rebecca and her family believed God was in it and they were willing to let her go to a far distant land with a man they had never previously met.

The story of this servant's sign from God was also something that Isaac could have for full assurance that the one he married was God's perfect choice for him. Today we know people who fear they married out of God's will and struggle with fears that things will never work out well for them. Isaac never had that problem, because God had revealed His perfect will through the sign.

JACOB'S LADDER TAKES HIM TO A HIGHER LEVEL OF FAITH

Jacob was presumably a believer in Jehovah God before his "Open Heaven" vision. However, after God revealed Himself to Jacob and spoke His promises to him, Jacob found himself not just believing in God, but he also became extremely committed to God. He first set up a memorial pillar and poured oil over it. Second, he renamed the city, "House of God" (Bethel). And third, he vowed to tithe all of his income if God would keep him from harm.

It is significant to point out that Jacob did not just see angels going up and down the heavenly ladder. At the top of the ladder Jacob saw the Lord Himself. God spoke to him and renewed the covenant He had made with Abraham and Isaac. **It was not the angels that impacted Jacob the most, but His encounter with God Himself.**

The angels, however, were a sign that God was interacting with His children on the earth. They were carrying out their assignments from God and returning to Heaven for their next divine mission. The sign of the angels gave Jacob added confidence that what God was promising, He would do.

Thus, Jacob was given encouragement for his faith through both the sense of sight and the sense of hearing. He saw the angels and the ladder and the glory of God at the top. But he also heard the voice of God which further activated his faith.

JOSEPH'S SPIRITUAL GIFTS IMPACT THE THEN-KNOWN WORLD

As we move on to the incredible story of Joseph, we discover again the power of the supernatural to create faith in people. Because Joseph had correctly interpreted the butler's dream while in prison, the butler believed that he could interpret Pharaoh's dream as well.

When Joseph revealed the meaning of Pharaoh's dream correctly, Pharaoh believed in the power of His God. Because of the power to interpret dreams, Joseph was able to be an incredible witness to the Egyptians and to all the people of the surrounding nations, who came to Joseph for food during the famine.

Since most of the then-known world had to come to Egypt for food, we can easily imagine that people from many nations came to believe in the God of Joseph. For example, imagine the talk in the palace of the King of Ethiopia.

Let's set the scene. The Ethiopian foreign minister, Rashib Hassahm enters the palace and proceeds to the throne room of King Morahem. He is obviously excited about something.

THE MYSTERY OF THE EGYPTIAN GRAIN SUPPLY

RASHIB HASSAHM: "Your Highness, I have heard that there is still grain in Egypt."

KING MORAHEM: "Do you have that from a reliable source?"

RASHIB HASSAHM: "Yes, Your Majesty. Our own ambassador just sent a report."

KING MORAHEM: "Well, that is very good news. We have had no crop for two years now. Have the Egyptians had rain?"

RASHIB HASSAHM: "No, Your Highness. The drought continues in Egypt as well."

KING MORAHEM: "Then how is it that they still have grain?"

RASHIB HASSAHM: "They have a Hebrew governor, named Joseph, who prophesied the famine nine years ago, and all Egypt began to save grain during those prosperous seven years."

KING MORAHEM: "A Hebrew, did you say? And what gods does he worship?"

RASHIB HASSAHM: "They worship the Lord Jehovah, whom they say is the Creator of everything, and the only true God."

KING MORAHEM: "Oh yes, I've heard that they have an unusual religion. But if their God has prepared them for this famine, we must learn more about Him. Send a delegation immediately. Tell them to buy grain and to learn more about this Hebrew God. None of our own gods have ever prepared us for a coming famine like their God. And be sure to send a generous gift to the Hebrew governor. See that the gold and silver we send are the highest quality in all the land of Ethiopia."

44

RASHIB HASSAHM: "Yes, Your Majesty. As you have spoken, so shall it be done."

When foreigners, like the Ethiopians, arrived in the land, they would seek to communicate with Joseph or his brothers, who helped him distribute and sell the grain. They surely must have been impressed with the stories told of Joseph's earlier dreams, his interpretation of dreams in prison and his rise to power under Pharaoh. And many must have been convinced that the Lord Jehovah was truly the one true God.

CHAPTER 4

Coming to Faith: The Mosaic Record

A PEOPLE WAIT IN BONDAGE FOR A SIGN OF HOPE

The section of scripture we are about to explore is one of the most exciting portions of Scripture we will be privileged to examine. Here we will see the dynamic impact of signs and wonders. Here the divine purpose and plan of God for signs and wonders will be graphically revealed.

When Moses came on the scene in the land of Egypt, the people of God had little memory of their spiritual heritage. We have limited knowledge of how much they believed in the God of Abraham, Isaac and Jacob. We know the Pharaoh of Moses' day had little knowledge of Joseph or his God, and we know the people were burdened down in slavery and had not seen much evidence that their God was with them.

At the very least, they needed a fresh dose of faith to believe that God could deliver them from their bondage. Today, like then, there are so many people all around us who are enslaved in all kinds of fetters and chains. They are waiting for someone who can show evidence that there is a God who both cares enough and has power enough to deliver them from their evil taskmasters. From the story of Moses we can learn the principles of deliverance for ourselves and also for them.

THE MYSTERY OF THE BURNING BUSH

In the final two verses of Exodus 2, we read that God heard the groaning of the children of Israel, and that He remembered His covenant with Abraham, Isaac and Jacob. We also learn that He looked upon the children of Israel and acknowledged them.

In the first verse of Exodus 3, we read that Moses "led his flock to the back of the desert, and came to Horeb, the mountain of God." This was a prophetic act, even though Moses didn't realize it at the time. Later he would lead his new flock, the children of Israel, to this mountain, where they would be nourished by the word of God, given through Moses.

In Exodus 3:2, Moses sees the sign and wonder of the burning bush. It was a wonder because it made Moses wonder, "What in the world is going on here?" It was a sign because it was saying, "God can use anything, including a desert bush to get people's attention, by setting it on fire, without it getting burned up."

Later, Moses was to become a burning bush himself. His face would glow as if it were on fire, and everyone would see it as a sign that Moses had been with God.

God began to lay on Moses an awesome destiny calling, but Moses could not believe he could fulfill it. So God immediately gave him a series of signs to stimulate his faith, which was very weak at the time.

The first thing God said was,

*"I will certainly be with you. And this shall be a **sign** to you that I have sent you; When you have brought the people out of Egypt, you shall serve God on this mountain." (Exodus 3:12)*

After more instructions from God, Moses asked,

"Suppose they will not believe me or listen to my voice; suppose they say, 'The Lord has not appeared to you.'" (Exodus 4:1)

Is this not the trouble we have when we try to convince people of God's love for them? So many people who are sincerely seeking truth still have doubts when we witness, because of past experiences where God didn't rescue them when they needed help. What was God's answer to Moses' honest question?

God's Prescription for Belief – Special Signs

God responded by telling Moses to cast his rod on the ground. When it became a snake and almost gave Moses a heart attack, God told him to pick it up by the tail and it became a rod again.

Then God said,

> *"**That they may believe** that the Lord God of their fathers, the God of Abraham, the God of Isaac, and the God of Jacob, has appeared to you." (Exodus 4:5)*

This was clearly a sign for God's people, not for religious hypocrites. The people were skeptical, but not anti-God. God wanted them to believe and gave them a sign that they could see with their natural eyes to help them believe.

Then God told Moses to put his hand in his bosom and take it out. It became white with leprosy. He repeated the process and it became normal again.

Then God made the powerful declaration:

> *"Then it will be, if they do not believe you, nor heed **the message of the first sign**, that they may believe **the message of the latter sign**. And if they do not believe even these two signs, or listen to your voice, that you shall take water from the river and pour it on the dry land. And the water which you take from the river will become blood on the dry land." (Exodus 4:8,9)*

What compassion and patience God had for His people. He prepared three signs just to convince His own people that He loved them and had come to deliver them. Today God still has compassion and patient understanding for people who have never had someone demonstrate the love of God to them in a supernatural way.

Next, God commands Moses to show these signs and wonders before Pharaoh as well. Even though Pharaoh's heart would be hardened, perhaps God's purpose was for the whole court to see His awesome power.

After these instructions, God orchestrates a meeting with Aaron. Then Moses tells him what God has spoken and shows him all the signs God has given him to do. After seeing the signs, Aaron believes and goes with Moses to meet with the children of Israel.

Now please read the following Scripture carefully with heart and spirit wide open to the voice of God.

> *"And **Aaron spoke all the words** which the Lord had spoken to Moses. **Then he did the signs** in the sight of the people. **So the people believed;** and when they heard that the Lord had visited the children of Israel and that He had looked on their affliction, **then they bowed their heads and worshipped."** (Exodus 4:30,31)*

Moses and Aaron did two things:

1. They spoke the words of God.
2. They did signs to confirm the word.

Does this not sound like Mark 16:15-20? Jesus commanded them to preach the word and promised that supernatural signs would follow believers when they preached. The concluding verse of Mark's gospel declares,

> *"And they went out and preached everywhere, the Lord working with them and confirming the word through the accompanying signs. Amen." (Mark 16:20)*

It seems to me that God had not changed His basic pattern of making believers from the days of Moses to the days of the early church. Perhaps it is time again to make a strong appeal to God to bring us back to His pattern, no matter how much of our own tradition we have to leave behind.

We stated that Moses and Aaron did two things. They spoke the word, and did signs to confirm the word. But the children of Israel also did two things in response to the preaching accompanied by the signs.

1. They believed.

2. They worshipped.

Is there anything we want more than those two things when we evangelize? Our goal should always be to bring people to faith and to bring them into a relationship with Jesus that will cause them to worship Him with all their hearts.

From this point on in the Mosaic record we have a continuous series of signs and wonders performed with the express purpose of producing faith. As stated earlier, the plagues in Egypt were repeatedly called signs and wonders.

For example, note the words of the Lord to Moses in Exodus 10:1,2.

> Now the Lord said to Moses, "Go in to Pharaoh; for I have hardened His heart and the hearts of his servants, that I may show these **signs** of Mine before him, and that you may tell in the hearing of your son and your son's son, the mighty things I have done in Egypt and My **signs** which I have done among them, that you may know that I am the Lord."

Note that the purpose for showing the signs was that the Children of Israel and their children and grandchildren would know that their God was the Lord. In other words they would more readily believe in Him because of these signs.

Pharaoh and his cohorts did not become believers in the God of Moses, because of the hardness of their hearts, not from lack of proof of His power. Pharaoh and company, like the Pharisees of Jesus day, were not seeking for truth, but for the perpetuation of their status and power.

We also discover that the Children of Israel quickly forgot previous signs and were inclined to succumb to fear and panic when a new challenge appeared on the scene. But God, knowing where they were coming from, was very patient with them, and demonstrated His power over and over to them.

There came a time however, that God became more and more angered at their lack of faith, especially since He had shown them His signs and wonders so abundantly. But here again, He made it clear that the signs and wonders were for the purpose of building their faith.

GOD EXPECTS PEOPLE TO RESPOND TO HIS SIGNS WITH FAITH

Note the following passage in Numbers 14:11:

*And the Lord said to Moses: "How long will these people reject Me? **And how long will they not believe Me, with all the signs which I have performed among them?***

In other words, "I gave you my signs so you would believe, but even with all these signs you still don't believe Me." The context of this verse is the failure of the people to believe that they could go into the Promised Land and conquer the giants. They were not very spiritually sensitive and so God had given many signs for their natural senses. But even that did not keep their faith strong.

Now we could argue that in the light of this occurrence, the signs and wonders were just temporary props for their faith. If these miracles didn't get them through the next trial, what good were they?

The answer is that without the signs and wonders, the Israelites wouldn't have even given Moses a chance. They would also have never crossed the Red Sea, and they would have turned back to Egypt for good. Their children would never have entered the Promised Land and none of the blessings would have been available to them.

Signs then, are not the object of our faith, but they are a powerful catalyst to faith. When God shows His power, it is easy to believe in Him. There are often times when our faith is tested. Miracles may be held back in order to draw us into a deeper intimacy with Him, but that will usually end up producing a higher level of faith.

Again, faith grows with increased revelation of the person we want to believe in. That revelation can be either to the natural senses, as with signs and wonders, or it can be to the spiritual senses that come when we draw near to Him in prayer and worship and in partaking of His Word.

LACK OF INTIMACY = LACK OF FAITH

Israel, as a nation, could have had that intimate relationship that would have made their faith strong, but they were afraid to get too close to God. They asked Moses to talk to God on their behalf and then tell them what God wanted them to do. It is so much easier to just follow rules than it is to ascend the mountain of God ourselves and risk being turned into "crispy critters" because of the brightness of His glory.

Moses, however, basked in the glory of God and hungered for much more. As a result, he had one of the most interesting and intimate encounters with God that any earthling ever had. God allowed him to see the back part of Him, but would not let him see His face. The biblical record tells us that God made known His acts unto Israel, but He made known His ways to Moses.

The greatest place in God is not the place where God is doing signs for us continually to build our faith. Rather the greatest place in God is where we have His heart for the lost and unbelieving and can be used by Him to produce signs and wonders that build the faith of the seeker, whose faith is weak or non-existent.

CHAPTER 5

Coming to Faith: Joshua Through the Kings

If only God would give us more detail. But Joshua 1:1 simply states that, "The Lord spoke to Joshua the son of Nun, Moses' assistant, saying:"

The first nine verses of the book of Joshua record the commission of God to Joshua, which encourages him to be courageous and lead the people into the "promised land". We don't know if Joshua heard an audible voice, was visited by an angel, was spoken to by a prophet, or if he just heard a still, small voice in his spirit. But somehow, God got the message across to him.

Joshua obviously was stimulated in his faith and immediately commanded his leaders to prepare to cross over the Jordan River.

THE FAITH OF RAHAB

The biblical record of Rahab, the harlot, reveals the power of supernatural signs and wonders to cause many to believe in our God. Listen to her testimony in Joshua 2:9-11.

"I know that the Lord has given you the land, that the terror of you has fallen on us, and that all the inhabitants of the land are fainthearted because of you. For we have heard how the Lord dried up the water of the Red Sea for you when you came out of Egypt, and what you did to the two kings of the Amorites who were on the other side of the Jordan, Sihon and Og, whom you

*utterly destroyed. **And as soon as we heard these things, our hearts melted; neither did there remain any more courage in anyone because of you, for the Lord your God, He is God in heaven above and on earth beneath.***"

Unfortunately for the rest of the inhabitants of the land, they did not come to saving faith. But they were convinced that the Hebrew God was the true God, and this belief came because of the miracles that were reported to them. But the wickedness of the inhabitants was so great that God had determined to remove them from the land which He had ascribed to His chosen people.

But Rahab, the harlot, requested to be saved and God granted her request. The crimson thread was placed in the window and her life was preserved, along with the lives of her whole family.

CROSSING THE JORDAN

In Joshua 3:7 God says to Joshua, *"This day I will begin to magnify you in the sight of all Israel, that they may know that, as I was with Moses, so I will be with you."* God then gives Joshua instructions for crossing the Jordan.

Joshua spoke to the people according to the information he had received, *"By **this** you shall know that the living God is among you, and that He will without fail drive out from before you the Canaanites and the Hittites and the Hivites and the Perizzites and the Amorites and the Jebusites."*

The **"this"** he is referring to is the SIGN that God promised do for them when the priests put their feet in the Jordan. He tells them that the water of the Jordan will part as soon as the soles of the feet of the priests get wet at the edge of the river.

PUPOSE AND POWER OF THE SIGN

This sign of the parting of the Jordan was clearly given, according to Joshua, for the purpose of producing faith in the hearts of the Children of Israel that God would also drive out the enemy from the Promised Land. Every time they faced a battle, wondering if they were able to defeat their enemy, they could look back to the day that they crossed the Jordan with the waters piled up in a heap far upstream.

One Israeli soldier would say to the others, "Remember when we crossed the Jordan? Joshua told us before we crossed that river that God would part the river as a sign that He would drive out all the nations of the land before us."

Another would answer, "That's right! How could we ever forget the Jordan drying up? One minute the water is flooding the land all around the river and the next minute it looks like there hasn't been rain for six years, it's so dry."

A third soldier would chime in, "So what are waiting for? The city is ours! Come on guys, let's roll."

And thus we can see once again how God gave His children visible signs for their natural senses that would reveal His power and glory to them for the purpose of giving them more faith in the times when their faith would be challenged. But there was another benefit of this miracle sign. Joshua 5:1 declares:

"So it was, when all the kings of the Amorites who were on the west side of the Jordan, and all the kings of the Canaanites who were by the sea, heard that the Lord had dried up the waters of the Jordan from before the children of Israel until we had crossed over, that their heart melted; and there was no spirit in them any longer because of the children of Israel."

BENEFICIAL SIDE-EFFECTS OF GOD'S SIGNS

The second benefit of the miracle sign was that it put fear into the heart of the enemy. When the enemy sees that God is with us because He is performing awesome signs and wonders among us, it puts a powerful fear into him. This is chiefly because he knows that we are encouraged in the Lord and discovering who we are in the Kingdom of God.

When we know deep down in our heart that God is with us,

there is nothing the enemy can do to us. Most of what he gets away with is a result of our lack of awareness of our own authority over him. That is why he fears the worst when signs and wonders begin to happen in the church.

He knows that faith in God will skyrocket and his attempts to plant doubts and fears will not work because God's people have seen a mighty miraculous sign right before their eyes. Instead, he himself, becomes filled with fears and doubts about his own ability to deceive the people of God.

GIDEON SEEKS A SIGN
and another sign
and another sign
and another sign

The next clear episode where we find someone going from unbelief to faith is found in the book of Judges. In Judges 6:11, we read that the Angel of the Lord came and sat under a terebinth tree while Gideon was threshing wheat. It's interesting to picture an angel just sitting under a tree, watching a young and fearful Israelite threshing wheat in the winepress to hide his harvest from the oppressive Midianites.

After an unknown lapse of time the Angel of the Lord appears to Gideon and speaks to him saying, *"The Lord is with you, you mighty man of valor."*

Gideon seems unfazed by the fact that the Angel of the Lord has appeared to him. He obviously thinks he is just a stranger in the area. As a result, he begins to challenge the statement made by the angel.

"And Gideon said to Him, 'Oh my lord, if the Lord is with us, why then has all this happened to us? And where are all His miracles which our fathers told us about . . .'" Judges 6:13a

Notice the fact that Gideon wants to know why they haven't seen the miracles of the kind that he has heard about from his fathers. This reveals that the stories of signs and wonders were still having some effect, but the people had not seen much of the supernatural in their own generation. Of course, they had forsaken God and served other gods, which explains why they hadn't seen many signs and wonders.

In the following verses the Angel of the Lord continues to speak encouraging words to Gideon. He tries to convince him that God has called and equipped him to deliver the Children of Israel from the Midianites, in response to their cries for deliverance. Gideon protests that he is the "least of the least" in Israel and not able to deliver them from Midian.

In verse 17, after the Angel of the Lord insists that God is with him and he will be victorious, Gideon decides to stop arguing, and asks for a sign that will prove that the angel is really the messenger of the Lord. The angel complies and causes fire to rise up out of the rocks to consume the sacrifice that Gideon had prepared. Then the angel does a vanishing act and Gideon goes into shock.

It is only at this moment that Gideon realizes that he has been talking to the Angel of the Lord. Now he fears for his life, having seen the Angel of the Lord face to face. But the Lord speaks to him again. We don't know if He reappears to Gideon or speaks to him in an audible voice from Heaven. At any rate, He lets Gideon know that he won't die and that he has nothing to fear.

The Lord continues to talk to Gideon and gives him instructions to cut down the altar of Baal and the image beside it. He must then build an altar and sacrifice a bull to the Lord, using the wood from the image he is to cut down.

Gideon gets 10 of his father's servants and obeys the Lord, using the cover of night, again out of fear. But this time it is the fear of his own father's household and the men of the city. They were obviously still into the worship of Baal, even though the people had been crying out to the Lord for relief.

Gideon is still a little timid, but it is clear that his faith in God has grown immensely after seeing the first sign performed by the Lord. It gave him the courage to obey the Lord and risk his life. Indeed, the men of the city came to Gideon's father to demand that he be put to death. Fortunately, Joash, his father, came up with a great line of defense when he said, "If Baal is a god, let him plead for himself."

So Gideon passed the first test of faith and obedience, and then the Spirit of the Lord came upon him. He blew the trumpet and gathered men from all the neighboring tribes. But now the real test was to come. The Midianites, along with the Amalekites, were gathering together to quickly quell this potential uprising.

At this juncture Gideon felt the need for another shot in the arm as far as his faith was concerned. He had never in his brief lifetime even thought of doing what he was about to do. He felt as if he was hanging by his fingernails on the edge of a cliff. Recognizing his fear, he asks God for another sign.

Gideon respectfully asked God for a wet fleece on dry ground. God complied without complaining. But Gideon still felt insecure and asked God to repeat the sign in reverse. Again God patiently and willingly responded.

After three supernatural signs Gideon was feeling a lot stronger in his faith, but let's notice something very important to our study hear. **Not only was God not angry with Gideon for asking for three different signs, but God offers him one more encouragement in the form of a fourth sign.**

GOD ENCOURAGES GIDEON TO SEEK A FOURTH SIGN

In Judges 7:9 God exhorts Gideon to attack the Midianites, but offers him one more sign, in case he was still a bit fearful and lacking in faith. Gideon accepts this offer and sneaks into the enemy's camp to overhear the conversation of two soldiers. One shares a dream and the other interprets the dream. The interpreter declares that Gideon the son of Joash is going to defeat them through the power of God.

Finally Gideon has seen and heard enough and his faith has risen to a high enough level to attack with his little band of 300 men. The small size of Gideon's army was the result of God's desire to make the victory another miraculous sign to the Children of Israel.

Like Moses, and the Children of Israel in Egypt, Gideon needed a lot of encouragement before he was willing to risk his life and defy a powerful foe. But God again was very patient and accommodating. It is a blessing to know that God knows our frailty and is not going to desert us the first moment our faith flounders.

RUTH – THE MOABITE BELIEVER
No direct signs and wonders needed

We don't know much about Ruth and how she came to be a believer in the God of her husband's family, but it's obvious that she did become a believer through her statement to Naomi, "Your people shall be my people and your God, my God."

The most likely scenario is that she heard the family talking about their God and all the wonders He had done for them. The Israelites, like all nations in those days would tell the stories passed on from generations to their children and grandchildren. And God had specifically commanded them to do so in regards to the mighty works He had performed in their midst.

But perhaps the biggest influence in the life of Ruth to make a believer out of her was the life and character of the family she had become a part of. **We must never lose sight of the fact that there are people who can be brought to faith through a loving witness.** While we want to make a case for the power of signs and wonders to create faith, we are not going to lose sight of the fact that a certain percentage of people in the world can be reached with a sincere and loving witness.

Not all people need to see signs and wonders to believe, even though these supernatural events can cause their faith to be stronger. But the fact is there were a few people, like the foreigner from Moab, who are just looking for a loving and godly example to convince them that there is a God who really does love them. For some souls, the fact that someone loves them can be a miracle in itself.

Personally, I believe that Ruth's faith was the result of a combination of the loving witness of her family and the testimony that the Hebrews traditionally shared about the miraculous power of their God. Probably she compared the lack of exploits of her own gods and the lack of character and love of the people who worshipped those gods with what she had seen in her new family.

SAMUEL'S PROPHETIC VOICES KEEPS ISRAEL FOCUSED ON GOD

During the days of Samuel, we don't read of any unbelievers becoming believers as such, but we do see the prophetic ministry of Samuel convincing men of God's call on their lives. First, it was Eli, the priest, who believed the warning of God through the child, Samuel, even though he didn't do much about it.

After that Samuel is able to convince a reserved and shy Benjamite, named Saul, that God has chosen him to be king. He prophesies several things to Saul that quickly come to pass and Saul becomes another man.

Later, Samuel would come to the house of Jesse to find the proper replacement for Saul. David, the shepherd boy, was prophetically chosen from among Jesse's sons and was anointed by Samuel to be the future king of Israel.

During the reigns of Saul and David, Samuel helped the Children of Israel keep their faith in God through his prophetic ministry. Like a circuit rider, Samuel moved about the country, encouraging the people to follow God, using his prophetic gift to bring encouragement and correction when needed.

GLORY DAYS OF DAVID AND SOLOMON

We read of no miraculous signs and wonders during the reigns of David and Solomon, except for battle victories and the prophetic ministry. Numerous prophets ministered to David and to Solomon, giving them advice and correcting them when they erred. David showed God's power with miraculous victories over enemies like the Philistines, including Goliath. Through these victories David helped to keep the faith of the Children of Israel strong.

David's military exploits, which depended on the wisdom and help of his God, did attract attention and respect among the surrounding nations. He did make some friends, such as Hiram, king of Tyre, who would later help Solomon build the temple. We don't know if Hiram became a believer in the God of Israel, but he certainly had a great love for David, according to I Kings 5:1.

SOLOMON'S WISDOM IS A WITNESS TO THE NATIONS

In the days of Solomon, as a result of the great foundation that David had laid for Solomon's kingdom, and the supernatural gift of wisdom that God had given to Solomon, people from many nations came to Jerusalem to check out what they had heard. It appears that many of them did become believers. FirstKings 10:24 puts it this way:

"And all the earth sought the presence of Solomon to hear his wisdom, which God had put in his heart."

As in the days of Joseph when the whole world came to Joseph for food, people from all nations came to Jerusalem to hear about the God of Israel, a God who could raise up a king with such incredible wisdom and administrative skill.

Notice now in I Kings 10:6-9, the words of the Queen of Sheba who was given a complete royal tour of all of Solomon's glory.

"It was a true report which I heard in my own land about your words and your wisdom. However I did not believe the words until I came and saw it with my own eyes; and indeed the half was not told me. Your wisdom and prosperity exceed the fame of which I heard. Happy are your men and happy are these your servants, who stand continually before you and hear your wisdom! Blessed be the Lord your God, who delighted in you, setting you on the throne of Israel! Because the Lord has loved Israel forever, therefore He made you king, to do justice and righteousness."

In my mind there is no doubt that every visitor was told about the living God, who had given Solomon this supernatural gift of wisdom to rule God's people as he had asked when given the opportunity. And then it must have been explained that God gave Solomon all the riches and glory in response to his "Kingdom First" prayer which he had made to God.

Thus there were probably many converts to the God of Israel through the reigns of David and Solomon. These occurred without the more visible, tangible signs and wonders, but rather through the glory that God brought down on those who served Him with love and loyalty.

APPLYING THE SOLOMON EVANGELISM PRINCIPLE

A good conclusion to draw from this time in Israel's history is that the unbeliever can be attracted and convinced to respond by the believer's success in the material realm, if the glory and credit go to a supernatural God. Our God honors those who honor Him. For the sake of winning souls, or making believers of those impressed by financial success, we can be a sign and a wonder. We can do this if we give God control of our finances and our business, and give Him all the honor and glory for our success.

Of course, many would love to be the one to witness in this manner. Maybe you, the reader, are praying right now, "God, just make me rich and I'll tell everyone about You and Your power." Unfortunately, many Christians have neither the character to build riches, nor the discipline to use them wisely, should they receive such blessings. It is however, a great blessing to hear the testimonies of men who are truly being used by God to reveal the wonders of God's divine principles of success and prosperity.

Certainly, God wants to reach all levels of society and He can use more people in this category as well. It's not a selfish thing to want to reach leaders and successful businessmen for Jesus. God will use many in this way in the days ahead, not only to be a strong testimony to the upper class of society and government, but also to help finance the end time harvest.

ELIJAH AND ELISHA BRING FAITH TO BACKSLIDDEN ISRAEL

As we have just noted, not many miraculous signs and wonders were recorded in Scripture during the reigns of David and Solomon, when the people of Israel were already walking in faith. But under the ministries of Elijah and Elisha, the miraculous signs and wonders came back in force. Their appearance on the scene came after the northern tribes had been led back into idolatry by their leaders.

Elijah comes on the scene during the reign of Ahab and prophesies a drought, the length of which will be determined by his own word. Then he hides by a brook and is fed by ravens. When the brook dries up, he finds a widow and son about to eat their last meal. He asks for the first plateful and then performs a miracle. The result is a continuous replenishment of the widow's flour and oil.

When the widow's son gets sick and dies, the prophet prays life back into him. It is at this point that we have a declaration of a newly-acquired belief that Elijah is indeed a man of God. First Kings 17:24 declares:

> *Then the woman said to Elijah, "Now **by this I know** that you are a man of God, and that the word of the Lord in your mouth is the truth."*

She obviously already believed in God, but her faith in the man of God was not too solid. The miracle convinced her that he was just that. Perhaps there had been so many false prophets serving the backslidden king that she was skeptical. We certainly have similar problems with people not believing us today because of previous bad experiences.

But wouldn't it be great to have people say to us what the widow woman said to Elijah. It would make it a lot easier to minister the truths of God's word, if people had no more doubt about our sincerity or the anointing on our lives.

Decision Time on Mount Carmel

Elijah's greatest miracle, which produced the greatest results, was calling down fire from Heaven on Mount Carmel. The fire burned up the sacrifice and proved that the Lord was the only true God. Let's notice the prayer that Elijah prayed in I Kings 18:36, 37, before the fire fell.

*"Lord God of Abraham, Isaac, and Israel, **let it be know this day that You are God in Israel**, and that I am Your servant, and that I have done all these things at Your word. Hear me, O Lord, hear me, **that this people may know that You are the Lord God,** and that You have turned their hearts back to You again."*

Elijah's heart was for God to bring His people back to Himself. He wanted the people to know that the God of their fathers was still their God and that He still cared about them and that he (Elijah) was God's servant, simply doing what God had told him to do.

In other words, **the purpose of the sign from Heaven was to make the people believe again in God**. Now let's look at the results of this sign in I Kings 18:39.

Now when all the people saw it, they fell on their faces; and they said, "The Lord, He is God! The Lord, He is God!"

God answered Elijah's prayer! A back-sliding nation repented on their faces and confessed that the Lord was their God. This is one of the greatest examples in all of Scripture, that signs and wonders can bring many people to radical faith in a very short time.

Elisha's Double Portion Anointing

Elisha was used by God to perform more recorded miracles than anyone else in the Old Testament. From parting the Jordan, after watching Elijah ascend in a whirlwind, to raising a dead man with his own dead bones, Elisha moved in miracles continuously.

Many of his signs and wonders were to solve local problems, with the obvious result that people's faith in God was strengthened and encouraged. For instance, he raised a lost ax head out of the water; he multiplied the oil to help a widow woman pay her debt; he fixed a pot of food that had poison in it so it could be eaten; he revealed to his king where the enemy was going to attack next thus saving the nation from military defeat; and he raised a child to life to bring joy to a grieving mother. (Read II Kings 2-6)

But again we find that it was when the man of God had an encounter with a foreigner that we find the strongest statement of saving or conversion faith. The miracles done among his own people were no doubt great encouragements to their faith, but we want to look at the transformation that took place in the heart of a heathen general, an enemy of the Children of Israel.

THE CONVERSION OF NAAMAN

Naaman was, as we read in II Kings 5:1, a commander of the army of the king of Syria. He was a mighty man of valor, but he was a leper. The Syrians were the chief enemies of Israel at the time, and he would not have been a welcome friend of the Israelites.

But his wife's young Hebrew slave cared about Naaman and knew about Elisha. She told her mistress that the prophet in Samaria could heal Naaman of his leprosy. Here again, we discover that **the fame that follows a man of signs and wonders will open the door for future witness about the power of God.**

Hearing this, Naaman told his king, who sent him to the king of Israel with a letter asking him to heal Naaman of his leprosy. This put the fear of God into the king of Israel, who ripped up his clothes, and declared that the Syrians were looking for a quarrel.

Fortunately Elisha heard the news and told his king to send Naaman to his house. When Naaman arrived, Elisha sent out a messenger to tell him to take seven dips in the dirty Jordan River. Naaman was insulted that Elisha wouldn't come to him in person, given his status. Only after his servants begged him to obey was he willing to humble himself in this foreigners' river.

When Naaman came out of the water with skin like a baby's, he became an instant believer in the God of Israel. Listen to the words of his mouth recorded in II Kings 5:15.

"Indeed, now I know that there is no God in all the earth, except in Israel; now therefore, please take a gift from your servant."

In addition, Naaman apologized in advance for the occasions when he would have to accompany his king into the temple of Rimmon and bow down with him. Elisha told him to go in peace and rejected any reward for his services.

Through the wonderful healing miracle, Naaman converted from his heathen gods to the God of Israel. He was committed to serve God and was very likely a powerful witness in Damascus. Most likely the whole nation along with his friends and acquaintances heard about the amazing miracle and the power of the God of Israel.

NINEVAH BELIEVES THROUGH JONAH

One of the greatest and most interesting Bible stories is that of the ministry of Jonah to the people of Nineveh. Jonah 3:5 declares:

"So the people of Nineveh believed God, proclaimed a fast, and put on sackcloth, from the greatest of them to the least of them."

The Bible doesn't give the details as to the reason the people repented, but many speculate that Jonah had been discolored by the stomach acids of the great fish that had swallowed him up and spewed him back out on the shore. Many scholars feel that this had a great impact on the people.

It is also likely that he was asked why his skin was such a strange shade of green. It is also probable that he shared his fresh testimony of God's dealings with him and how God showed mercy in giving him another chance. Accordingly then, it would make sense that the people of Nineveh would also hope for the same mercy from God, and that they would also take seriously the warning of impending judgment.

In other words they were thinking something like this: "If God is that hard on His own prophet, then He might do worse to us." On the other hand, "If God was merciful to him and gave him another chance, than maybe He will give us another chance as well."

It was not likely that the people would believe a foreign prophet unless there was something very unusual about him. It is interesting to think of the possibility that the consequences of Jonah's initial rebellion against God's command (causing his skin to turn green in the whale's belly) actually helped to bring repentance to the people of Nineveh. And that was the one thing that Jonah didn't want to happen.

But they did repent and God changed His plans for destroying the city. Jonah, of course, did not approve of God's ways, and had a big pity party. But it was in all likelihood that because Jonah became a living sign and a wonder, the people believed the word of the Lord.

Another interesting side-note here is the fact that the word of the prophet did not come to pass. He specifically prophesied that the city had only 40 days before destruction would come. Many critics of prophecy quote the law of Moses, saying that such prophets are false prophets and would have been stoned.

The ironic thing is that Jonah wanted to die when his prophecy did not come to pass. But God would not let him die, much less be stoned by the people.

It is clear that our actions can affect the fulfillment of prophecy. Or in other words, prophecies, whether positive or negative, can be conditional on the obedience or disobedience of the recipients.

REVIVALS UNDER GREAT KINGS

While the northern kingdom of Israel slipped deeper and deeper into heathenism after the departure of Elijah and Elisha, the southern kingdom of Judah and Benjamin experienced many wonderful revivals. These took place basically as a result of several very strong and godly leaders that took the throne in those days.

Both Solomon's son, Rehoboam, and his grandson, Abijah, went through times of backsliding and were not the strong leaders that

Judah needed to keep them from idolatry. A lot of idol worship had come in to compete with the worship of Jehovah.

ASA AND JEHOSHAPHAT

But Asa, the son of Abijah, sought the Lord and began to cleanse the land of evil and idolatry. His son, Jehoshaphat, also walked with God and continued the fight against heathenism in the land.

Both of these leaders experienced major miraculous victories in battles against their enemies. These victories involved earnest prayer, listening to God's strategic instructions conveyed by prophets, and singing worship songs on the battlefield.

The miraculous victories against huge armies, which resulted from listening to the prophets, were the only recorded signs and wonders during this period of time. We also have no record of any individuals coming to faith during this era. It seems obvious, however, that many who were taking part in idolatry came back to the God of Abraham, Isaac and Jacob.

HEZEKIAH RECEIVES A MIRACLE DELIVERANCE

The next outstanding king of Judah was Hezekiah. He had followed a mixed bag of kings, some were part-time God-serving kings and some were quite wicked. Hezekiah began an energetic restoration of temple worship and facilitated a great revival in Judah. We are told in II Chronicles 29:3 that he began the restoration in the very first month of his reign, while he was a mere 25 years old.

He restored the temple completely, brought back Davidic worship, and celebrated the Passover feast with great festivities. And everything Hezekiah did was prosperous, because he did it with all his heart (II Chronicles 31:21).

But Hezekiah also faced a very powerful enemy, who came to conquer Jerusalem and to take all its best citizens back to Assyria. Like Asa and Jehoshaphat, he prayed to the Lord and listened to the prophet that God had given him. And like his forefathers, he obeyed the voice of the Lord and rested in His promises.

The result of Hezekiah's trust in God, through the word of the prophet, Isaiah, was that the angel of the Lord killed 185,000 Assyrians, without any help from the army of Israel. This was another powerful sign that God was still a miracle working God, and that He would be their deliverer if they put their trust in Him.

We can easily imagine the encouragement this was to the faith of the Israelites. But we can also be confident that the nations all around heard about this great miracle. After all, the Assyrians were conquering country after country, and had become the dominant power in the then-known world. And yet a little nation like Judah had sent them home with their tails between their legs. God's reputation surely grew on the earth through such a wonderful and miraculous victory.

JOSIAH LEADS THE LAST GREAT PRE-EXILIC REVIVAL

The last great king of Judah was Josiah, who also brought great revival to Judah. Hezekiah's son, Mananasseh, had a long and very wicked reign. His grandson Amon had a very short, but equally wicked reign. But his great grandson, Josiah turned his heart passionately to the Lord. He cleansed the land and held a tremendous feast at Passover. The people rejoiced and worshipped their God.

Unfortunately for Judah, Josiah didn't wait to be attacked by a foreign power. Instead, he got proud and thought he could take on Necho, king of Egypt, who was at war with Carchemish, by the Euphrates. When Necho suggested that Josiah not mess with him, Josiah didn't take his advice and was soon hit by an archer's arrow. He died shortly thereafter.

It was the last hurrah for Judah. After this event Judah was controlled and dominated first by Egypt and then finally by Babylon. King Nebucadnezzar hauled off everything and everyone worth his effort to Babylon, which is modern Iraq.

Josiah had the opportunity to follow in the footsteps of Asa, Jehoshaphat and Hezekiah, who saw awesome miracles of deliverance to confirm the faith of their people. But because of his pride, the revival he had begun fizzled and the opportunity to rekindle the faith of his people was lost.

King Ahaz Refuses to Ask for a Sign

Before we move on to the period of the captivity, we should mention one other story that we referred to in an earlier chapter. King Ahaz of Judah was not a godly king, but he did have the prophet Isaiah to help keep him in line. In Isaiah 7, Ahaz finds himself threatened by the combined armies of Syria and the northern tribes of Israel. He and his people begin to tremble in fear for their lives.

But God quickly sends Isaiah to meet with King Ahaz with a word from God. The message was "Be quiet and fear not." God would once again show His people His power, so they would believe in Him.

To prove His power, God invites King Ahaz to ask for a sign from God. He could ask for a sign in the heavens or in the earth. But Ahaz refuses, saying, "I will not ask, nor will I test the Lord!" (Isaiah 7:12).

But God is not pleased with Ahaz's refusal and accuses him of wearying God. He then goes on to give Ahaz a sign, whether he wants one or not. The sign is the famous prophecy that a virgin would conceive and bear a Son, whose name would be Immanuel.

This of course, had a fulfillment in Ahaz' day, as well as in the miraculous birth of Jesus. The Hebrew word used here for virgin can mean either a young woman or a literal virgin. Thus it was the perfect word for two different kinds of fulfillment.

The important point with regards to our study is that God wants to prove Himself to those who are uncertain about whether to believe in Him or not. Rather than being offended by those who asked a sign, He welcomed them to do so. Only the religious leaders in Jesus days were criticized for asking for a sign, and that was only because of their hypocrisy.

CHAPTER 6

Coming to Faith: Daniel and Friends

The book of Daniel is full of evidence that miraculous signs and wonders can produce faith in those who are total unbelievers. Much of the miraculous in this book has to do more with the prophetic than with physical, visible signs and wonders.Other miracles were miracles of protection. However, as we shall see, all of the above produced the desired results.

KING NEBUCHADNEZZAR'S DREAM

Nebuchadnezzar, the mighty and ruthless emperor, who had conquered most of the then-known world, had a dream which greatly troubled him. Instead of sharing the dream with the magicians, the sorcerers, the astrologers, the Chaldeans, and the other wise men to interpret it, he demanded that they reveal the dream itself and then provide the interpretation. The result of failure to describe the dream would be death to the whole lot of them. In fact, the king was very graphic about their death. They were to be cut in pieces and their houses made an ash heap.

Not one of the psychics in the whole group had any idea what the dream was about, and they made strong protests to the king that he was being unreasonable. They obviously didn't like the consequences for failure that he had decreed. They could dream up an interpretation if he first shared the dream, but no one had ever asked them to first furnish the dream and then interpret it. But Nebuchadnezzar was determined to follow through with his command and his prescribed punishment.

Daniel and his three friends, Shadrach, Meshach and Abednego, happened to be four of the "wise men" in the land. When Daniel heard the news he suggested that everyone relax a bit and he would seek the Lord his God. With his friends joining him in prayer, Daniel sought the Lord. God revealed the secret in a night vision (Daniel 2:19) and Daniel reported the good news to the king.

After revealing to the king his vision of a huge statue, which was prophetic of present and future kingdoms, Daniel interpreted the dream to him. The results were not only gratifying, but literally amazing.

Here was the most powerful human being on the earth. But with nothing more than a word of knowledge through a vision and interpretation, this powerful monarch fell at Daniel's feet and

". . . commanded that they should present an offering and incense to him." (Daniel 2:46)

Then Nebuchadnezzar made the following statement to Daniel:

"Truly your God is the God of gods, the Lord of kings, and a revealer of secrets, since you could reveal this secret." (Daniel 2:47)

This powerful statement of belief brought favor to the children of Israel who were living in Babylon, the land of their captivity. Following this verse we read,

"Then the king promoted Daniel and gave him many great gifts; and he made him ruler over the whole province of Babylon and chief administrator over all the wise men of Babylon." (Daniel 2:48)

The next verse declares:

"Also Daniel petitioned the king, and he set Shadrach, Meshach, and Abed-Nego over the affairs of the province of Babylon; but Daniel sat in the gate of the king." (Daniel 2:49)

Thus, we see that not only did the king believe, but the servants of God were given high honor and prestige, **simply because of a supernatural gift of God.**

FOUR MEN IN THE FIRE

Unfortunately, Nebuchadnezzar had a short memory and in the next chapter we find him making a huge golden image, probably about 90 feet high, and commanding everyone to worship it. It is important to note that there may have been many years between the events of chapter two and chapter three.

But however long it was, the king was now worshipping idols again. It was the normal thing to do in his culture and tradition. But God was about to remind him that He was still God. When his decree went out that everyone must bow down and worship, there were three Hebrew young men that wouldn't bow. They were Daniel's three friends. Obviously, Daniel was out of town when the idol dedication took place.

The king was furious and ordered his men to heat the furnace seven times hotter. We know the story. The three Hebrew men were joined by a fourth, whom the king described as appearing like the Son of God. The fire was certainly hot enough, as it killed the men throwing them in the furnace. It was also hot enough to burn the rope that had them bound, but it wasn't hot enough to burn their flesh or their hair, because God had shielded them from the heat of the fire.

Now please notice the words of Nebuchadnezzar in Daniel 3:26:

"Shadrach, Meshach, and Abed-Nego, servants of the Most High God, come out, and come here."

Because of the miracle, the king recognized that their God was **the Most High God.** He goes on to say before many of the rulers of Babylon in Daniel 3:28,29:

"Blessed be the God of Shadrach, Meshach and Abed-Nego, who sent His Angel and delivered His servants, who trusted in Him,

and they have frustrated the king's word, and yielded their bod-
ies, that they should not serve nor worship any god except their
own God! Therefore I make a decree that any people, nation, or
language which speaks anything amiss against the God of
Shadrach, Meshach and Abed-Nego shall be cut in pieces, and
*their houses shall be made an ash heap; because **there is no other***
God who can deliver like this."

NEBUCHADNEZZAR LEARNS HUMILITY

The third chapter of Daniel concludes with the declaration that
the three Hebrew young men were promoted in the province of
Babylon. Chapter four begins with a proclamation of Nebuchadnezzar
to "all peoples, nations and languages that dwell in all the earth:"
Verse two and three proclaim,

*"I thought it good to declare the signs and wonders that the **Most***
High God** has worked for me. **How great are His signs, and
***how mighty His wonders!** His kingdom is an everlasting*
kingdom, and His dominion is from generation to generation."
(Daniel 3:2,3)

The king had learned a lot by now and his faith, like Gideon's
was stronger now than after the first miracle. However, he still had a
problem with pride and when he boasted about what he had accomplished in Babylon, God brought him very low. He became insane
and lived like a beast for seven years, just as Daniel had prophesied.

The end result was that Nebuchadnezzar became a humble servant
of God. Notice the maturity in him in Daniel 4:34-37.

"At the end of the time I, Nebuchadnezzar, lifted my eyes to
heaven, and my understanding returned to me; and I blessed the
Most High and praised and honored Him who lives forever: For His
dominion is an everlasting dominion, and His kingdom is from
generation to generation.

All the inhabitants of the earth are reputed as nothing; He
does according to His will in the army of heaven and among

*the inhabitants of the earth. No one can restrain His hand or
ay to Him, 'What have You done?'*

*At the same time my reason returned to me, and for the
glory of my kingdom, my honor and splendor returned to me.
My counselors and nobles resorted to me, I was restored to my
kingdom, and excellent majesty was added to me.*

***Now I, Nebuchadnezzar, praise and extol and honor the
King of heaven,*** *all of whose works are truth, and His ways
justice. And those who walk in pride He is able to abase."*
(Daniel 4:34-37)

Once again we have seen the progression of faith corresponding
to the progression of signs and wonders in someone's life. The three
major miracles in the king's life brought him to the place of true
worship, and the recognition of the greatness and character of God.

It would be easy to criticize and say that his faith didn't last, after
the first sign from God. That was true, but Daniel and his friends
were faithful to keep a pure testimony and they continued to minister in God's supernatural power. The result was the complete conversion of the man who wielded the greatest political and military
power in the world.

BELSHAZZAR SEES THE WRITING ON THE WALL

Nebuchadnezzar's son, Belshazzar, didn't learn from his father
the value of humility and the power of God to correct a proud man.
As he partied with his lords and ladies, and drank wine from the
holy vessels from Jerusalem; and as they all praised the gods of human
creation, God's finger began to write Belshazzar's judgment on the
wall.

When none of the king's psychics could interpret the writing, the
queen reminded Belshazzar about a man named Daniel, who was
trusted by his father, and had in him an excellent spirit to interpret
dreams, etc. The king quickly sent for him and promised him great
riches, if he could interpret the writing on the wall.

In spite of the very negative and judgmental interpretation given by Daniel, the king still gave Daniel great honor and promotion in the kingdom. However, he didn't get to enjoy the promotion for too long, as Belshazzar was slain that night and Darius, the Mede took his throne.

Although there was no great expression of faith by Belshazzar, the prophetic sign was a witness to all who were in the king's court. Those who survived the overthrow of his kingdom would know that Daniel's God was the only power in the kingdom who could both write and interpret the sign of the handwriting on the wall.

DARIUS LEARNS A LESSON FROM LIONS

Darius, the Mede, loved Daniel and made him one of the top three men in the empire. Because of the "excellent spirit" in him "he distinguished himself" above the others and the king was planning to put him over the whole realm of his kingdom.

This stirred the jealousy of the other governors and satraps, who came up with a plan to get Daniel in trouble. They appealed to the king's pride and devised a scheme that would get Daniel out of the picture before it could get painted.

Their plan seemed to be working. Daniel right on cue, and without hiding or hesitation, prayed three times a day as he always did, even though the king had signed the decree that no one could ask petitions from any god or man other than him alone. Daniel's faith and courage revealed a very intimate relationship with God. His spiritual senses were probably as sharp as any saint in Scripture other than Jesus, Himself.

Darius realized too late that he was caught in the trap because of his own pride. Daniel 6:14 says that he *was greatly displeased with himself."* However, he followed through with his signed and sealed edict, and had Daniel thrown into the lion's den. At the same time he said to Daniel, *"Your God, whom you serve continually, He will deliver you."* (Daniel 6:16)

He was exercising what faith he had, but he couldn't sleep that night. He rose early and called down into the den with the question:

"Daniel, servant of the living God, has your God, whom you serve continually, been able to deliver you from the lions?" (Daniel 6:20)

Of course, we know that God did indeed deliver Daniel, and that his accusers, with all their families, were cast into the lions' den. The lions were starving by this time and made short work of Daniel's enemies.

But Darius learned his lesson and once again a reigning monarch over all the nations of the earth sent a decree saying:

"To all peoples, nations, and languages that dwell in all the earth; Peace be multiplied to you. I make a decree that in every dominion of my kingdom men must tremble and fear before the God of Daniel. For He is the living God and steadfast forever. His kingdom is the one which shall not be destroyed, and His dominion shall endure to the end. He delivers and rescues, **and He works signs and wonders in heaven and on earth,** *Who has delivered Daniel from the power of the lions. (Daniel 6:25-27)*

Darius learned that God was stronger than the lions. His faith had been weak but after the miracle deliverance from the lions, his faith rose to a new level. And Daniel just kept on serving the Lord and prospering. He was a foreigner and a captive, but he was given honor and power in the courts of the emperor.

We can only speculate, but it seems reasonable to assume that because of Daniel's respected position in the empire, and because of the supernatural gifts that he possessed, that many people, besides the kings, were brought to believe in the God of Daniel.

Daniel continued to prosper throughout the rest of the reign of Darius and then also in the reign of Cyrus, the Persian (Daniel 6:28). Cyrus became a tool in God's hand to begin the restoration of Judah and Jerusalem. Perhaps it was through the influence and the testimony of Daniel that he made the decree that Jews could return to the land of their fathers. If that were true, than the signs and wonders done through

Daniel had a much greater impact than we have given them credit for.

We must remember that **no matter how much character and spiritual fruit Daniel had, and how great a leader he was, he would still not have outlived the reign of King Nebuchadnezzar without the supernatural revelation gift that He had from God. Instead he would have been killed along with all the Babylonian psychics, and the same fate would have happened to his three Hebrew friends.**

RESTORATION PROPHETS STIR UP FAITH

There is clear evidence from the books of Ezra, Nehmiah, and the final four Old Testament books that the prophets played a large role in helping the people restore the Jerusalem Temple and the city walls. The people were afraid of their enemies and the commandment of the emperor, and they quit building what God had told them to build.

Their faith was obviously very weak, but when the prophets and other leaders began to encourage them, their faith was strengthened and they returned to their task. Notice the following Scriptures:

"Then the prophet Haggai and Zechariah the son of Iddo, prophets, prophesied to the Jews who were in Judah and Jerusalem, in the name of the God of Israel, who was over them. So Zerubbabel the son of Shealtiel and Jeshua the son of Jozadak rose up and began to build the house of God which is in Jerusalem; and the prophets of God were with them, helping them." (Ezra 5:1,2)

"So the elders of the Jews built, and they prospered through the prophesying of Haggai the prophet and Zechariah the son of Iddo. And they built and finished it, according to the commandment of the God of Israel . . ." (Ezra 6:14)

"Then Haggai, the Lord's messenger, spoke the Lord's message to the people saying, 'I am with you, says the Lord.' So the Lord stirred up the spirit of Zerubbabel the son of Shealtiel, governor

*of Judah, and the spirit of Joshua the son of Jehozadak, the high
priest, and the spirit of all the remnant of the people; and they
came and worked on the house of the Lord of hosts, their God."
(Haggai 1:13,14)*

These passages clearly show that the faith of the people was
strengthened through the prophetic message given by various prophets. This may seem like a less powerful form of the supernatural, but
its impact can often be every bit as powerful as a visible supernatural
sign.

A BRIEF SUMMARY OF OUR RESEARCH IN THE OLD TESTAMENT

From Adam to Daniel, we have discovered that God was more
than willing to show His power through signs and wonders for the
sake of producing faith in His people and in foreigners as well. The
Israelites actually didn't have any idea how much God wanted to
reveal Himself to the whole world.

At the beginning, people could know about God through Adam,
who had walked in the garden with God. God also revealed Himself
to people, such as Abraham and Moses more directly, and they heard
His voice speaking to them. Often God used angels, some of whom
were apparently in the form of people. But they communicated God's
words to His children. Thus faith in many Old Testament folks came
through hearing the "rhema" word of God.

For those with difficulty believing, such as the Israelites in Egypt,
and Gideon, God was very patient, giving them several signs to build
their faith. There were others, like Solomon, who were given gifts of
wisdom and knowledge in order to reveal the greatness of God to
them, and to those who would encounter them.

Ruth and others probably came to faith, not by seeing the miracles,
but rather by hearing about them and observing the consequences
of lives that were dedicated to God. Some men like Elijah brought
down fire from heaven or performed other miraculous wonders so
that whole nations would turn to the living God.

So far in our research, we have found clear statements in Scripture that signs and wonders were given for the purpose of producing faith. We have also found many examples to prove that the miracles did produce the desired results.

On the other hand, we have found very few examples of people who came to faith without witnessing a supernatural event, and these were probably influenced by the stories of God's miracles. In several places in the Old Testament we read the commandment God gave the Israelites to pass on the stories of His awesome miracles to future generations, so that they too would believe in the Lord their God.

We have also discovered that people often did forget the miracles, and as a result, their faith quickly faltered. We learned that God wanted a relationship with people, which would keep their faith strong. Signs and wonders would help, but a child of God should not continually need them to sustain his or her own faith.

The signs and wonders are performed so that we are convinced of the reality of the invisible God. But God does want us to develop spiritual senses so that we can know Him on a much deeper level.

As the Scripture says, God revealed his acts to the Children of Israel, but He revealed His ways to Moses. Through intimacy, Moses learned God's ways. But most of the Children of Israel never did get intimate with God to learn His ways, and as a result, their faith was continually wavering.

We have also seen that prophetic gifts, such as those possessed by Joseph and Daniel could have the same witnessing power as the miraculous or healing gifts. They were also signs and wonders to kings and rulers.

With that preliminary summary, let us now proceed to the New Testament, where we can study the words and practice of Jesus, Himself, and the apostles of the Lamb who followed in His footsteps.

CHAPTER 7

The First Believers in Jesus

ANGELIC APPEARANCES FOSTER FAITH
IN VARIOUS CHOSEN VESSELS

The coming of Jesus to the world was the most incredible event that had ever taken place in the whole course of human history. It was a crucial historical marker in the Father's eternal time-line. It was a time when the spiritual forces were lining up for battle for the hearts of men. The Spirit of God would once again hover over the earth, and the spirits of darkness would once again try to bring chaos, confusion and control over the minds of men.

God didn't leave anything to chance. He knew well His agenda and the fact that His Son would be the sacrifice for the souls of men. He had His mightiest angels prepared for their assignments. Gabriel, the chief messenger angel, would prepare the chosen vessels with special visits on the earth.

Every one of these angelic visits was to produce the belief that the Messiah was on the way. They would be the first people to put their faith in Jesus as their Savior and Lord.

ZACHARIAS GOES DUMB

The first person to be visited by Gabriel was a God-fearing older priest named Zacharias (Luke 1:1-80). He was busy performing his priestly duties when Gabriel appeared to him on the right side of the altar of incense. He was troubled and fear came upon him, but Gabriel said "Fear not!"

Then Gabriel told him that his wife Elizabeth would give him a son in her old age. He would be a special vessel to prepare the way of the Messiah. When Zacharias was hesitant to believe, the angel gave him a sign to stimulate his faith. The sign was that he would have "acute laryngitis" until the day of the birth of his son, whom he would call John. He was not able to speak again until John, the Baptist, was born, and he had written his name for others to read.

Because of this sign and the words of praise that Zecharias spoke after his voice was restored, the people around him also believed that God was preparing them for the coming of the Messiah. Luke declares:

> *"Then fear came on all who dwelt around them; and all these sayings were discussed throughout all the hill country of Judea. And all those who heard them kept them in their hearts, saying, 'What kind of child will this be?' And the hand of the Lord was with him." (Luke 1:65,66)*

Then Zecharias was filled with the Holy Spirit and prophesied over his son, declaring the coming of the Messiah to bring salvation and light to those who sit in the shadow of death. This prophetic word was another revelation from God that was designed to encourage the faith of all those who could hear that their Messiah was coming soon.

MARY RECEIVES HER UNUSUAL ASSIGNMENT

Gabriel's next assignment was six months later in Nazareth. But Mary, like Zacharias, was troubled by his appearance, and by his message to her. Again, Gabriel brings comfort and an explanation of God's desire and plan. Gabriel prophesies to her:

> *"The Holy Spirit will come upon you, and the power of the Highest will overshadow you; therefore, also, the Holy One who is to be born will be called the Son of God." (Luke 1:35)*

84

She was also told that her relative, Elizabeth, was five months pregnant, which was a miracle, because of her age. He reminded her that with God nothing was impossible. That was a truth that Mary also would have to believe to accept the message that Gabriel was giving her.

The words of Mary, which we could call her "Acceptance Speech" still stir my spirit, even as I write these words. She spoke the words that God desires to hear from each of us when He calls us and commissions us. After hearing Gabriel's amazing announcement she simply replied:

> *"Behold the maidservant of the Lord! Let it be to me according to your word." (Luke 1:38)*

Thus faith came by hearing for Mary. The supernatural appearance of Gabriel left no doubt in Mary's mind that this incredible event was about to happen. She was about to become the most privileged woman to have ever lived, and at the same time she would become one of the most misunderstood. Getting pregnant before marriage was a major disgrace in those days for any normal gal. And how many would believe if she did try to explain it?

LITTLE JOHN DOES JUMPING JACKS IN THE WOMB

As soon as Mary heard the news, she hurried from Nazareth to a city of Judah, where Elizabeth and Zacharias lived. The moment that she entered the house and greeted Elizabeth, little baby John, the Baptist, did the "Holy Ghost Hop" in Elizabeth's womb. Now Gabriel had prophesied that John would be filled with the Holy Spirit, "even from his mother's womb." So it really was possible that he was manifesting the Spirit of Joy.

In fact, Elizabeth herself was filled with the Holy Spirit (Luke 1:41) at the moment when Little John leaped in her womb. The infant prophet couldn't lay hands on her head or shoulders to impart the Holy Spirit, but he found a way to make the presence of the Holy Spirit felt from within.

But the important point for our study is that through this sign and wonder, Elizabeth became a believer in Jesus, possibly even before He was conceived. She blessed Mary and called her "the mother of my Lord."

Mary responded in the spirit of grace and magnified the Lord with a beautiful monologue known as "The Magnificat". Although some religions may have exalted Mary above measure, there is a virtue and grace about Mary that is an awesome example to us of a true servant of the Lord. She knew how to humbly receive the blessings of God, and she knew how to meditate and ponder things in her heart, rather than proclaim to everyone how important she was.

JOSEPH HAS ANGELIC DREAMS

While Matthew doesn't tell us the name of the angel, he tells us three times than "an angel of the Lord" appeared to Joseph in a dream (Matthew 1, 2). In the other angelic visitations mentioned above, Gabriel actually appeared to the people he spoke to. But Joseph was a dreamer who got his direction from the Lord while he slept.

The first dream revealed that Mary was pregnant by the Holy Spirit and her son would be named Jesus, "for He will save His people from their sins." In the second dream the angel told Joseph to take his family to Egypt to escape Herod's sword.

While in Egypt, Joseph received instruction from the angel to return to Israel because Herod was dead. All of these major decisions were directed by angelic visits as Joseph slept. Certainly, these supernatural events reaffirmed the faith of both Joseph and Mary as they fulfilled the incredible responsibility of raising the very Son of God.

SHEPHERD'S ENJOY A LATE-NIGHT CONCERT

Humble shepherds, taking care of their sheep in the hills of Judea, were treated to an unexpected concert by a host of heavenly visitors, who praised God saying, "Glory to God in the Highest, and on earth peace, good will toward men."

But before the multitude of angels appeared, we read:

"an angel of the Lord stood before them, and the glory of the Lord shone around them, and they were greatly afraid." (Luke 2:9)

This angel spoke to them about the birth of a Savior, who was their Christ and their Lord. Then the angel told them,

*"And this will be the **sign** to you: You will find a Babe wrapped in swaddling cloths, lying in a manger." (Luke 2:12)*

The shepherds didn't ask for a sign, but the angel gave them an additional sign to the ones they had already seen. The appearance of the angel and the glory of God shining upon them should have been sign enough. In addition, a host of angels appeared in the sky praising God. But God wanted them to have no doubts when they found the child, so He added one more sign for a clincher.

God revealed His love and His understanding of the weakness of man's faith. He still does the same today. He gave Gideon four signs; He gave the children of Israel many more and if we are honest with ourselves, we know that He has given us our fair share of miraculous signs and wonders.

Personally, I can say that God has done many miracles for us, especially in the area of provision. And yet, like many others, we find ourselves anxious and fearful when the next crisis threatens. But if we recall and rehearse in our minds the miracles of the past, it builds our faith for the present miracles that we need.

WISE MEN BELIEVE GOD'S SIGNS

Wise men always believe the signs that God shows them. The famous magi from the east were no exception. Somehow they were given the ability to understand that an unusual star in the sky was a sign from Heaven that a very special King was born in the land of the Jews.

The wise men came seeking to worship the new King, which is what wise men still do. When they saw the star again, it led them right to Jesus. But after they had worshipped Him, they received a warning from God in a divine dream and did not return to Herod, who had only pretended that he also wanted to worship the new King. When he realized that the wise men had slipped away without giving him the information he desired, he slaughtered all the baby boys in Bethlehem under two years old.

Herod was another person, like the Pharisees, who had evidence that Jesus was the Son of God, but who was fearful of losing his power. He tried to use the wise men like the Jews used Judas to betray Jesus. But Jesus' time had not come and His mission had not been fulfilled.

SIMEON BELIEVES THROUGH DIVINE REVELATION

Simeon was a resident of Jerusalem who was "just and devout". God chose him to be a recipient of a revelation of the incredible event which took place in Bethlehem. On the eighth day after Jesus' birth, Mary and Joseph came to Jerusalem to present Jesus to the Lord, and to have Him circumcised according to the law of Moses.

Simeon was waiting for Him, having heard from the Holy Spirit that he would not see death until he had seen the Messiah. I love Luke's description:

"So he came by the Spirit into the temple." (Luke 2:27)

Simeon walked in the Spirit. What an example for us! Here is an Old Covenant saint who had a personal intimate relationship with the Holy Spirit and moved by the voice of the Holy Spirit.

Simeon not only walked in the Spirit, but he was blessed to have a special encounter with the newborn Messiah. Simeon may have waited many years for the fulfillment of the promise, but as he walked in the Spirit faithfully, the exciting day finally came. It may seem like a long wait for many who seek the Lord, but I believe that all those who are faithful to walk in the Spirit will, like Simeon, have some very special encounters with their Messiah and Lord.

Simeon not only received the blessing, but he was also used to minister a blessing to Mary and Joseph and Baby Jesus. He prophesied the ministry of Jesus; that it would not only be to the glory of His people, Israel, but also a light to bring revelation to the Gentiles. Today, He is still bringing light and revelation to the Gentiles, and we are still benefiting from the fulfillment of this prophecy of Simeon's.

ANNA CONFIRMS AND SPREADS THE NEWS

Anna was called a prophetess and was well over 100 years old. She had been married for seven years before she became a widow. Then she lived another 84 years before she "just happened" to be at the right place at the right time. She apparently lived in the temple and fasted and prayed night and day.

Luke tells us she came in at the instant that Simeon was prophesying and gave thanks to the Lord. Then Luke reports that she spoke of Jesus to all those who looked for redemption in Jerusalem.

The situation in Jerusalem reminds me of the situation in Christianity today. There are always plenty of religious people like in Jerusalem, but there are some who are not satisfied with religion as it exists, and are looking for a fresh visitation of the Lord. And as the Scripture says, "Those who seek will find." Anna shared her revelation only with true seekers, "those who looked for redemption in Jerusalem."

JOHN THE BAPTIST GATHERS BELIEVERS

John the Baptist, whose very conception was a miracle, became a literal sign and wonder to the nation of Israel. His life-style and bold ministry, along with the mission that he had in life, truly made him a sign to his people. When Jesus asked the Pharisees if John's ministry was of God or of men they couldn't answer Him for fear of the people. The people held him in great reverence as a prophet of God.

But John, himself, according to the people, did no miracle, but what he said about Jesus was true (John 10:41). John not only had many disciples who believed in him, but he spoke as a prophetic voice to introduce and proclaim Jesus as the "Lamb of God".

Belief Through the Power of the Anointed Word

Hear we can see a supernatural power to bring people to faith without physical or visible supernatural signs. It is the power of the prophetic word, and the power of influence of one who is perceived as a prophet. John had the prophetic anointing, which flowed through him and brought conviction to his hearers.

I believe we have seen a similar anointing on some evangelists, such as D. L. Moody and Billy Graham, to name just a couple. Without the persuasive power of miraculous signs and wonders, the power of God's anointing on their delivery brought the hearts of huge numbers of men and women to repentance and faith in Jesus.

But these and other evangelists who have possessed this power have invested much time in prayer in order that their words would be clothed in the power of the Holy Spirit. They have been called and chosen to speak like John the Baptist.

Their main calling is not to produce physical signs and wonders. They are called to do a wonderful work in the hearts of their hearers, and reveal to others the power to transform lives.

In other words, people don't just run up to the altars to confess faith in Jesus because of great logic or oratory skills, but rather because of the supernatural power of the Holy Spirit to bring conviction and faith into their hearts. Again, we are reminded that without the Holy Spirit drawing us and revealing Jesus to us, we could never even believe in Him.

John, the Baptist Prophet

John the (first) Baptist actually did not just speak with a strong anointing, even though the people said that John did no signs. He clearly manifested prophetic gifts. John 1 gives us several clear evidences of this fact.

In verses 26, 27 John prophesied that One much greater than he would follow him. In verse 29 he recognized Jesus for who he was through prophetic revelation. Then he prophesied that Jesus would be God's ultimate sacrificial Lamb that would take away the sin of the world.

He also had received a vision of the Spirit descending like a dove on Jesus and had been told prophetically that whoever the Dove descended upon would be the Son of God.

The result of this prophetic ministry was that his own disciples believed in Jesus and left John to follow the "Lamb of God." This is real evidence of true prophetic ministry.

A true prophet is not concerned with his own following. He is simply a messenger of a greater person. He cares that people believe in the word of the One who sent him.

John later made the commendable statement, "He must increase, but I must decrease" John 3:30. Let all prophetic people have the same goal in their ministry.

CHAPTER 8

Jesus Manifests Signs and Wonders to Produce Faith
(from John's Gospel)

JESUS' PUBLIC MINISTRY BEGINS

A s John passes the leadership baton to Jesus, we discover that Jesus begins His ministry the way that John was phasing out his own. John made believers in Jesus through prophesying to them.

Jesus made believers out of several of His disciples in the first chapter of John through His own use of prophetic gifts, without the benefit of the more physical and visible signs and wonders. The latter would not begin until chapter 2.

One of the first two disciples of John who transferred his allegiance to Jesus was Andrew. He immediately found his brother Simon Peter and brought him to Jesus.

When Jesus looked on him He said:

"You are Simon the son of Jonah. You shall be called Cephas."
(John 1:42)

First, Jesus tells him his name through a word of knowledge. Secondly, He prophesies that Simon's name will become Cephas. John doesn't tell us Peter's response, but we know he also became a disciple.

PHILIP HEARS A PROPHETIC COMMAND

The next day Jesus headed for Galilee and found Philip and said:

"Follow Me." (John 1:43)

This was what I call a "prophetic command." Jesus knew Philip would be a disciple and He was prophesying that Philip would become one of His faithful followers.

NATHANAEL, "THE SKEPTIC"

This was enough for Philip who went to find his friends, Nathanael. He tried to convince him that they had found the One who fulfilled the prophecies of Moses and the other prophets.

But Nathanael was not so easily convinced. He made the famous statement:

"Can any good thing come out of Nazareth?" (John 1:46)

Philip did the wise thing that any good evangelist will do and said:

"Come and see."(John 1:46)

Then Jesus demonstrated what to do when we face someone who is seeking the truth, but has been burned before by someone who is very zealous, but in error. Jesus didn't condemn him for his doubts, but rather complimented him for his character, using a prophetic revelation gift, which would fall into the category of a word of knowledge. Jesus said to him:

"Behold, an Israelite indeed, in whom is no guile!" (John 1:47)

Nathanael, "The Skeptic", quickly became Nathanael, "the Curious", asking Jesus where he got His information. Jesus then gave him the second word of knowledge, which He received through a vision. He declared to Nathanael:

"Before Philip called you, when you were under the fig tree, I saw you." (John 1:48)

94

Immediately "Nathanael, The Curious" becomes "Nathanael, The Convinced", and a total believer in Jesus, making the incredible confession:

"Rabbi, you are the Son of God! You are the King of Israel."
(John 1:49)

Jesus expressed admiration for Nathanael for believing with such limited evidence, but then He prophesied that Nathanael would see even greater things, including the heaven opening, and angels ascending and descending on Him.

Nathanael's story is very important to a proper understanding of faith. As we will see again in John 4, some people are harder to convince than others, but they are still willing to look at the evidence we have to offer. Jesus was patient and provided more evidence when a sincere person was not yet convinced.

I recall a situation in Argentina where a lady was coming forward for healing and then started to change her mind. My mentor, E. R. Burnette noticed her and asked her a question. He said, "Lady, if I can tell you your age, will you come forward for healing?"

He then revealed her exact age to the day. She came forward and ended up with a complete physical overhaul. Her husband was also healed of a double hernia that had almost incapacitated him.

The important point here is simply that some people need more encouragement than others to bring them to faith. This can come through additional signs or through prophetic gifts, such as a word of knowledge.

SIGNS BEGIN – MIRACLE RECHARGES FAITH OF DISCIPLES

In John 2, Jesus begins his miracle ministry, turning the water into wine. We know the story, but we need to focus on the comment after the story.

*"This beginning of **signs** Jesus did in Cana of Galilee, and mani-*
*fested (revealed) His glory; and **His disciples believed in Him**.*
(John 2:11)

We know the disciples already believed in Him or they wouldn't have been His disciples. But like the Israelites, and like all of us, without encouragement our faith begins to weaken.

But Jesus was on a campaign to reveal His glory to His own disciples and to His own people, to keep their faith strong and raise it to a higher level. This is what it's all about. We need to reveal the glory of Jesus, not our own glory, and people will believe in Him.

In verse 18 of John 2 the Jews asked Jesus what sign He would do since He had just driven out those who were making "His Father's house a house of merchandise." Jesus gave them the sign of "this temple" being destroyed and rebuilt in three days.Of course, He was referring to His own body being raised from the dead. After His resurrection His disciples remembered that He had prophesied this, and then we read:

*"and **they believed** the Scripture and the word which Jesus had said." (John 2:22)*

Verse 23 reports the following:

*"Now when He was in Jerusalem at the Passover, during the feast, **many believed** in His name **when they saw the signs** which He did." (John 2:23)*

This is another very clear statement about the power of signs to bring faith to those who seek to know the Truth.

But it is important also to notice Jesus' response to their faith. John comments:

"But Jesus did not commit Himself to them, because He knew all men, and had no need that anyone should testify of man, for He knew what was in man." (John 2:24,25)

The people believed in Jesus, but Jesus knew that their hearts were still fickle and that very possibly some of them would end up crying, "Crucify Him!" When I looked up the word for "commit" in the above verse, I was amazed to discover that the word is actually "believe."

The verse should really read, "But Jesus did not believe in them, because He knew all men." They believed in Him, because they saw His glory. He did not believe in them because He could see through them and saw their flesh.

He knew they would have to take the revelation of His glory and respond to it. The signs would help them believe. But they needed to grow in their faith and pursue God with pure hearts to develop their spiritual senses. Only then could they have a true relationship with God and worship Him in "Spirit and Truth".

A baby can be born and take its first breath, but if it is not fed and nourished, it will eventually stop breathing and die. We can see God's signs and wonders and be convinced that God is real, and then never nourish that faith with a relationship with Him.

The results will be the same. Our faith will die. I am not trying to address the issue of whether you can be lost after you have been saved.But I have certainly seen people who at one time had faith, but through neglect their faith became so weak it was almost non-existent.

Faith, as Jesus taught, is like a mustard seed. It is a small seed, but it has incredible potential for growth. But it must be given the correct environment, or it will never reach its potential.

So we must keep in mind this principle, as we continue to research the evidence, that faith needs not only to be "authored", but we need to remember the exhortation:

"looking unto Jesus, the Author and the Finisher of our faith."
(Hebrews 12:2)

We need to keep our eyes on Jesus, so he can finish or complete our faith in Him. Looking into His loving eyes, through the eyes of the Holy Spirit, we are encouraged to trust Him in any situation.

NICODEMAS REVEALS THE REASON FOR HIS FAITH

Nicodemas, a ruler and a Pharisee came to Jesus by night and made a profound statement as He began the conversation with Jesus. Under the cover of night, he had the boldness to declare:

"Rabbi, we know that You are a teacher come from God; for no one can do these signs that You do unless God is with him." (John 3:2)

Nicodemas said, "We know." This was a strong statement. And the "We know" was based on the fact that Jesus had done miraculous signs among the people. He was saying, "There is no way we can not believe in you, because we have seen these signs."

Another significant point is that he didn't say, "I know." He said, "We know." He was not the only one who believed because of the miracles Jesus did. We don't know if he was referring to other Pharisees, or the Jews, in general, but obviously there were many more besides himself that knew that Jesus was sent from God because of the great miracles they had witnessed.

This statement made by Nicodemas is another proof of the thesis we made earlier. The physical sign gives evidence to those who don't have their spiritual senses sufficiently activated to believe in God without that physical sign.

We can't have faith without a revelation of the person's faithfulness and character. And we cannot know God without spiritual senses activated, unless God has mercy and shows us His glory in the natural realm so we can see something with our natural senses.

God's will is for all of us to develop those spiritual senses, so our faith in Him can grow even in the seasons where we don't see the visible signs. These senses are alive, but they need to be exercised to become useful to us.

It is also important to remember that we should not be seeking signs exclusively for our own sakes, but we should be seeking signs for the sake of the non-believers who are open, but not yet convinced. The disciples prayed for signs and wonders to give them boldness to witness. We should do the same, for the sake of the Kingdom of God.

The rest of John 3 discusses the new birth and the fact that whoever believes in Jesus has everlasting life. That is why it is so important that we provide every opportunity for people to see evidence that Jesus is alive and able to do the impossible. Almost everyone has need of a miracle of one kind or another, and when they see a miracle, it can give them faith that their own need can be met.

SAMARIA BELIEVES AFTER ONE
PROPHETIC WORD OF KNOWLEDGE

The story told in John 4 is probably the single most dramatic biblical illustration of the power of the prophetic gift to bring people to faith in Jesus Christ. "The woman at the well" as the main character of the story is called, became an instant and powerful evangelist. This took place right after a conversation with Jesus that included a prophetic word of knowledge.

When Jesus told the woman she had already had five husbands and her present companion was not her husband, she was convinced that He was nothing less than a prophet. After Jesus plainly told her who He was, she immediately became an evangelist and ran off to the city to tell the men who were there.

John, the gospel writer, gives us the following description of their response:

"And many of the Samaritans of that city believed in Him because of the word of the woman who testified, 'He told me all that I ever did.'" (John 4:39)

Not only did the woman believe, but **the power of the prophetic word was extended via the testimony of the woman.** These people believed, according to the above Scripture, just because of her testimony.

Apparently some of the Samaritans were more like Nathanael, the skeptic, who had to hear Jesus for themselves. To them the woman had said,

"Come see a Man who told me all things that I ever did. Could this be the Christ?" (John 4:29)

The people of the city responded and John gives us the following report:

"And many more believed because of His own word. Then they said to the woman, 'Now we believe, not because of what you said, for we have heard for ourselves and know that this is indeed the Christ, the Savior of the world.'" (John 4:41, 42)

The "many more" that believed were the ones who wouldn't take someone else's word for it. They wanted to look more carefully at the evidence for themselves. Hearing Jesus speak His own words to them was enough to convince them that He was the Christ.

FAITH COMES BY HEARING

Jesus, of course, was a Prophet as well as every other gift-ministry listed in Ephesians 4:11. Everything Jesus said was prophetic in some way, because, as He declared, His teaching was not His own, rather it was the teaching of the One who sent Him. Prophecy is simply carrying a specific message from God to man for a specific situation in time and space. That is exactly what Jesus was doing every day.

What Jesus said always pierced the hearts of His listeners because His words were anointed by the Holy Spirit, Who knew the hearts of His particular hearers. The anointed word, as we have discussed earlier does have the power to convince or to produce true faith.

The Scripture makes it clear:

"Faith comes by hearing, and hearing by the Word of God."
(Romans 10:17)

By experience and as a result of extensive biblical research, I would add that the more prophetic or revelatory element there is in the word that comes forth, the more faith it will produce. For instance, the woman at the well was intrigued by this unusual Stranger, who made mysterious statements about "Living Water", but when He used a prophetic gift of knowledge, she was brought to a place of belief in what Jesus had to say.

To tie in this principle that faith comes by hearing the Word of God, we should remember that signs and wonders are not just a visible manifestation of an invisible God. As we discussed earlier, every sign must, by the very definition of the word, carry a message. A message is something that is verbal, which relates primarily to our sense of hearing, rather than to our sense of sight.

Signs begin as visible phenomena, but the significance of the sign is in the message we receive. It is very similar to reading the Bible. We use our eyes to receive the information, but the information becomes something we hear in our spirit. That is how faith comes by the Word of God. We hear the Word, as we read the Word.

THE NOBLEMAN GETS HIS SIGN AND BELIEVES IN JESUS

A certain nobleman had a son who was sick at Capernaum and heard that Jesus had returned to Cana of Galilee, where He had turned the water into wine. With his son at the point of death, he came in desperation to Cana to petition Jesus.

It was in this situation that Jesus made the statement,

"Unless you people see signs and wonders, you will by no means believe." (John 4:48)

Note: The NKJV inserts the word "people" after the words "Unless you," but the word "people" is not in the Greek text.

This statement by Jesus leaves no doubt as to the power of signs and wonders. He knew the weakness of people's faith and showed compassion not only on the nobleman, but on all those who watched. He wanted them to believe and was willing to show another visible sign to facilitate their faith.

If Jesus was expressing disapproval of the nobleman, it didn't stop Him from doing the sign. After the miracle took place at the same hour as Jesus said, "Your son lives", John makes the following statement:

*"And he himself believed, and his whole household. This again is the **second sign** that Jesus did when He had come out of Judea into Galilee." (John 4:53, 54)*

As usual, the message of the sign was that Jesus was their Messiah that they had waited for. The nobleman's whole household became believers in Jesus through this one great sign.

It should be mentioned here that the power of such a sign is not just a temporary thing. The fact is that this family would always have this wonderful testimony that Jesus had healed their son.

And the son, as he grew up would always know that Jesus was the reason that he was still alive. Throughout their lifetimes, I would expect that their story was told hundreds or even thousands of times.

Who knows the extent of the influence of one such miracle.

MULTITUDES FOLLOW JESUS BECAUSE OF SIGNS

In the sixth chapter of John we read this commentary:

*Then a great multitude followed Him, **because they saw His signs** which He performed on those who were diseased. (John 6:2)*

Obviously this great multitude was filled with people who believed in Jesus, at least at a beginning level of belief. They were there to hear the teachings of Jesus for just one reason – they had seen the signs that Jesus had done.

Even today, people come to hear the gospel in many nations, when they hear that miracles are taking place. There is no method of evangelism more effective or more biblical that using the miraculous to attract the unbeliever.

This is especially true in various mission fields. For example Reinhart Bonnke's ministry of miracles and healing in Africa draws enormous crowds that have yielded millions of decisions for Christ.

But this does not mean that the miraculous does not produce results in our western civilization. I have personally witnessed thousands of decisions for Christ in a couple of Benny Hinn services. The interesting fact was that the salvation invitation was given before the healing emphasis. Just the reputation of the evangelist's healing anointing gave credibility to his message, and led people to accept a transforming encounter with Jesus, which the evangelist proclaimed to be the greatest miracle of all.

MEAL MULTIPLICATION ON THE MOUNTAIN

But the gathering of the multitudes, who had come because of the miracles, created a new problem. The people had not planned on being gone from home so long, and had not prepared a picnic basket for the event.

As a result, Jesus felt compelled to feed them all. The men alone numbered 5,000. With the women and children there may have been three to four or five times that many.

Jesus calmly proceeded to use the sack lunch of the only lad who had brought one to feed the whole multitude. Five barley loaves and two small fish not only fed the multitude, but produced twelve baskets full of leftovers.

At the conclusion of this event John gives us this observation:

*"Then those men, **when they had seen the sign that Jesus did, said, 'This is truly the Prophet who is to come into the world."** (John 6:14)*

One powerful miracle sign made one powerful statement to those who observed it. They were very convinced that Jesus was the promised Messiah.

THE JEWS ARGUE ABOUT JESUS

By the seventh chapter of John, the opposition to Jesus by the Jewish leaders had gotten quite strong. Many people believed in Jesus but the religious heads were trying to make them afraid to proclaim it. John gives us the following statement, which clearly reinforces the thesis of this book:

*"And many of the people believed in Him, and said, 'When the Christ comes, will He do more **signs** than these which this Man has done?'" (John 7:31)*

The Jews clearly associated signs with the coming of the Messiah, which means "The Anointed One." Their whole tradition of faith was based on the fact that God had appeared to their forefathers and that many miracles had been done by the anointed prophets, which God had set among them.

BLIND MAN SEES AND REVEALS THE GLORY OF GOD

In the beginning of John 9, the disciples noticed a man blind from birth. When they asked Jesus whose sin brought on the blindness, Jesus said,

"Neither this man nor his parents sinned, but that the works of God should be revealed in him." (John 9:3)

The clear implication is that God had allowed this man to be blind for his whole life, in order that there be a revelation of Jesus' power. In other words, he would become a sign, to show the glory of God. Jesus came to reveal the glory of God through signs and wonders, and this man found out who Jesus was in a personal way.

Jesus made clay, spread it on the blind man's eyes and told him to go wash it off in the pool of Siloam. He came back seeing and created a big commotion among the religious leaders, who antagonistically interrogated both him and his parents. When Jesus heard that the man with new vision was cast out of the synogogue, He found him and asked him if he believed in the Son of God.

When the ex-blind man responded by asking Him who that might be, Jesus clearly told him Who He was. The man said"

"'Lord, I believe!' And he worshipped Him.'" (John 9:38)

Notice that he didn't just say that he believed, but he worshipped Him. His heart was overcome with gratitude and love.

Personally, I have no doubt that the faith of this man was very strong and remained strong for the rest of his life. He knew what the enemies of Jesus had done to him and he knew what Jesus had done for him. He knew what it was to be blind, and he knew the blessings of sight.

Those who have been spiritually blind and then receive clear spiritual sight are usually very committed and loyal to the One who has opened their eyes. It's those who think they see just fine without His help, that don't have a strong love for Jesus. Often they actually turn against Him by turning against His own people, and especially against those who love Him with a fervent, passionate love.

WORKS OF JESUS ARE FAITH-MAKERS

After teaching the people that He was the Good Shepherd, Jesus stirred up a major controversy as He talked about His Father, God. What followed was a big argument among the people that went like this:

"And many of them said, 'He has a demon and is mad. Why do you listen to Him?' Others said, 'These are not the words of one who has a demon. Can a demon open the eyes of the blind.'" (John 10:21)

Notice that those who believed in Jesus did not argue about His doctrine, as to whether it was biblical or not. They immediately referred to the visible, physical demonstrations of His power. In other words, the miracle sign was the message that He was from God and not from Satan. Indeed, have we ever seen a demon open the eyes of the blind?

Jesus then began to walk through the temple. The Jews in Jerusalem were getting impatient and wanted Him to publicly declare who He was. Jesus answered them like this:

*"I told you, and you do not believe. The **works** that I do in My Father's name, they bear witness of Me."* (John 10:25)

It was the works, or miracles, of Jesus that bore witness or spoke about Him. In other words, **the works were the signs** with a message that spoke about who Jesus was.

These Jews were not too excited about His answer and the other comments He made. They especially took exception to the statement He made that He and His Father were one. At that point they picked up stones to stone Him.

But Jesus just kept talking about the works or signs which He had done. He then went on to ask the people to believe in the signs and wonders if they had trouble believing in Him. He boldly declared:

"If I do not do the works of My Father, do not believe Me; but if I do, though you do not believe Me, believe the works, that you may know and believe that the Father is in Me, and I in Him." (John 10:37,38)

Jesus makes it very clear that He is trying to make it as easy as possible to believe in Him. Even if the Jews found it hard to believe His doctrine, He wanted them to believe the works themselves, because they were the signs from Heaven that He had come from Heaven.

Even with this appeal, the Jews tried to seize Jesus, but He escaped out of their hands. From there Jesus went to John's old stomping grounds near the Jordan and stayed there for a while. Then many people came to Him and declared:

*"John performed no **sign**, but all the things that John spoke about this Man were true. And many believed in Him there." (John 10:41,42)*

People were contrasting John with Jesus. They were verifying that John, although he, himself, did no signs, he was a true prophet, for he had predicted the works of Jesus. John had predicted a ministry of the Holy Spirit's fire and power and the people had seen it. There was a combining of the witness of John, the prophet, and the witness of the signs that Jesus did. The result was that many believed in Jesus. As in the days of Moses and Aaron, and the apostles in Acts, it was first the word, and then the signs following to confirm the word.

Slipping ahead to John 14, where Jesus is preparing His disciples for His death, He says to them:

*"Believe Me that I am in the Father and the Father in Me, or else believe Me for the sake of the **works** themselves. **Most assuredly, I say to you, he who believes in Me, the works that I do he will***

do also; and greater works than these he will do because I go to My Father." (John 14:11,12)

Anyone who reads the above passage and believes it to be true, must acknowledge that Jesus wants us to continue to produce the same kind of signs and wonders that He did. There was no indication that this was only for His disciples. Rather He said, "He who believes in Me." That includes us.

He introduced the statement, saying, "Most assuredly, I say to you." He wanted there to be no doubt about the truth of His words.

Later, after His resurrection, He would say:

*"These **signs** will follow those who believe: In My name they will cast out demons; they will speak with new tongues; they will take up serpents; and if they drink anything deadly it will by no means hurt them; they will lay hands on the sick, and they will recover." (Mark 16:17,18)*

Again, it says, "those who believe". It doesn't say "the apostles", or only those who live during the apostolic era, or before the Bible is completed. Jesus said emphatically, in two different times and places, "those who believe." I think that includes you and me.

But we must believe He wants to do it and has the power to do it. And we must want to see His signs for the right motive. Too many people want to produce the signs and wonders to get people to admire them.

Often people who start with good motives end up with motives that are less than pure as they get a taste of the attention they receive. The proper motive should be the same motive that Jesus had. He wanted the works or signs to prove that He had come from God.

As Jesus' body on the earth, and as His ambassadors to the earth, we want to prove that He is the Son of God, who came to the earth to bring salvation to a fallen race. We can best do that through the signs that carry the message that Jesus is still alive and showing his compassion and power to those in need.

LAZARUS – A PROPHETIC SIGN

The resurrection of Lazarus was the last great sign and wonder, which Jesus performed before His death. He clearly used it to reveal His power over death and to bring as many people to faith in Him as possible.

Jesus intentionally waited two days before He went to Bethany, where Lazarus was. He knew Lazarus was dying, but didn't want to get there too soon. He makes the reason clear:

*"Then Jesus said to them plainly, 'Lazarus is dead. And I am glad for your sakes that I was not there, **that you may believe.**'" (John 11:14,15)*

Jesus was not only trying to convince the common Jew, but He knew that He needed to continue to build a stronger faith in His disciples, because He was about to die and leave them alone for three days. He wanted them to have no doubt that He had all power over death.

When Jesus arrived in Bethany, He spoke to Mary and Martha about the fact that He was the Resurrection and the Life. He was also trying to get them to believe that He was more than a prophet, He was actually God come in the flesh.

When Jesus went to the tomb, after ordering the stone to be rolled away, He prayed specifically that people would believe that He had been sent by His Father. John reports the following events:

*"And Jesus lifted up His eyes and said, 'Father, I thank You that You have heard Me. And I know that you always hear Me, but because of the people who are standing by I said this, **that they may believe that You sent me.**' Now when He had said these things, He cried with a loud voice, 'Lazarus, come forth!'" (John 11:41-43)*

The whole purpose of His prayer was clearly to convince the crowd that He had been sent by His Father, God. But of course, the prayer by itself would not convince the people. It was the answer to the prayer that would confirm the words that He spoke to His Father.

In Mark 16, after Jesus spoke of the signs that would follow those who believe, Mark gives us the following report, which is also the conclusion to his gospel:

"And they went out and preached everywhere, the Lord working with them and confirming the word through the accompanying signs. Amen." (John 16:20)

Jesus confirmed His words to God with a sign. Later His disciples spoke the words and Jesus confirmed their words with similar signs.

When Lazarus came out of the tomb, Jesus told His disciples to loose him from his grave clothes. Then John informs us of the results of this miracle:

"Then many of the Jews who had come to Mary, and had seen the things Jesus did, believed in Him." (John 11:45)

They didn't believe because of His convincing words alone. They believed when they saw what He had done.

PHARISEES BELIEVE IN THE FAITH-MAKING POWER OF SIGNS

When the chief priests and Pharisees heard about the raising of Lazarus from the dead, they were very troubled. They gathered a council and said,

*"What shall we do? For this Man works many **signs**. If we let Him alone like this, everyone will believe in Him, and the Romans will come and take away both our place and nation." (John 11:47, 48)*

The anti-Jesus forces in Jerusalem were very aware of the "faith-making power" of the signs which Jesus did. They plainly stated that everyone would believe in Jesus if they let Him continue to perform these signs.

They clearly were not interested in the truth. They feared loss of position and power. Later, when the apostles were carrying on the work of Jesus, we discover the same reality. The council gathered together and said:

"What shall we do to these men? For indeed, that a notable miracle has been done through them is evident to all who dwell in Jerusalem, and we cannot deny it. But so that it spreads no further among the people, let us severely threaten them, that from now on they speak to no man in this name." (Acts 4:16)

Again they revealed their knowledge that the signs had the power to produce faith in the people who witnessed or heard about the signs. There will always be religious people who have too much to lose to accept a power that is not under their own control. But those who love God and His Kingdom will continue to seek to produce the signs and wonders to facilitate faith in the people who really want to know the truth.

JESUS PRAYS THAT THE WORLD WILL BELIEVE

In Jesus longest recorded prayer, found in John 17, we find Him praying for many things for His disciples, who will soon be without Him. He prays for their protection, for their sanctification, for His joy to be in them, for them to see His glory, and for several other things.

He prays only once or twice for any of those things, but He prays five times that His disciples may be one. This call for unity is much more fully addressed in my earlier book entitled, *"Heal Your Body, Lord"*.

Two of the five times Jesus prayed for unity, He gave us the reason for this prayer. **He prayed for unity so that the world would believe** that the Father had sent the Son.

At this point I would like to present what I believe to be a very important deduction from this prayer in the context of the rest of Scripture.

I believe that unity is a prerequisite for any significant release of power for signs and wonders. In answer to Jesus five requests for unity, we read five different times in the first five chapters of Acts (the fifth book of the New Testament), that the disciples were in one accord.

During these five chapters, we read that all kinds of wonderful signs and wonders took place. We read of an incredible healing line in which every single person who was sick or afflicted with demons was made completely whole. (See Acts 5:12-16)

In His prayer Jesus was clearly implying that if the disciples would be united, then the world would believe in Him. We have clearly shown that the more that signs and wonders were done, the more the people believed.

Thus I believe that Jesus was saying that if they would be united, then they would have more power to do signs and wonders, which in turn would bring people to faith in Jesus. When the unity began to weaken and divisions arose in the church, we find that not everyone was healed. Even though many miracles still happened, they did not come as easily as in the earlier days, when the church was in great unity.

For evidence of this change please check out the following Scriptures: I Timothy 5:23, II Timothy 4:20, Philippians 2:25-27.

THE THIEF AND BELIEF

We find two instances of people coming to faith during the crucifixion and death of Jesus. The first is the repentant thief who had a revelation that Jesus was indeed the Son of God, even though Jesus rejected the opportunity to come down from the cross and reveal His power in a convincing manner. We find this story in Luke 23:39-43.

In analyzing this story, I believe we can discover another effective way of convincing the unbeliever that Jesus is alive and real in our lives. To do so we need to back up to the verses just before those that tell us the story of the thief.

What the thief had just observed, prior to his rebuke of the other thief and his request for mercy, was a beautiful manifestation of God's mercy, forgiveness and love. Jesus had just had the nails pounded through His hands and feet. He had just felt the intense jarring pain as they dropped the cross into the hole in the ground. He had been listening to the mocking and cursing. He had seen the soldiers gambling over his robe.

But not one word of anger or hatred came out of His mouth. Not one curse or threat was released from His spirit. Instead, Jesus responded with the famous statement:

> *"Father, forgive them for they know not what they do." (Luke 23:34)*

The thief must have been amazed. This was not the normal response from a normal human being. I believe that the spirit of the thief was open, allowing revelation from God to come freely to him that Jesus was indeed the son of God.

Although we don't have many illustrations of this principle in the Word of God, we have seen some examples of similar responses when in somewhat similar situations. When the Holy Spirit inhabits our life and character, we sometimes find ourselves loving people who are attacking us and expressing hatred toward us.

It can also happen that people observe us when something bad takes place and we react with peace and tranquillity. I recall a time when some young converts went with me to a car auction. I had very little money and little experience at automobile auctions. I ended up getting a car I didn't really want, and spent more money than I felt that I could afford as a pastor of a small church on the coast of Washington.

About 25 miles or so down the road, the engine blew up and I had to arrange to have the car towed off the freeway. The young men watched my reaction, as I accepted my loss as a lesson learned, with trust in God that He would cover it.

One of the men expressed amazement that I was not expressing anger and losing my temper over the situation. It helped him understand that the Holy Spirit can change our nature when we allow Him to. It revealed to Him that Jesus really was alive. Although he was already saved, it put another leg under his table of belief in God.

EARTHQUAKE SHAKES DOUBTS, BUILDS FAITH

The last story of people coming to faith in Jesus before the resurrection, takes place at the time of Jesus' death. In Matthew 27:50-54, we read of a powerful earthquake that was interpreted by those who observed it as a sign from God.

As soon as Jesus had yielded His spirit to His Father, the veil in the temple split from top to bottom, as the earth quaked violently, even splitting rocks. Graves were opened and many dead saints came back to life and appeared to people in Jerusalem.

Among those observing this powerful earthquake was a Roman centurion and his soldiers. Matthew gives the following account:

"Now when the centurion and those with him, who were guarding Jesus, saw the earthquake and the things that had happened, they feared greatly, saying, 'Truly, this was the Son of God!'" (Matthew 27:54)

This was another special visitation from Heaven to reveal to those on earth the importance of the events which had just taken place. His birth, baptism, death, resurrection and ascension were all accompanied with major signs and angelic visitations.

The Father wanted to give everyone the evidence they needed to believe if they were truly seeking the truth about God. The Roman centurion and his soldiers, had observed Jesus on the cross. They may have heard his words of forgiveness and seen His meekness. Then they observed the powerful earthquake at His death and they knew this was not just another good man.

The supernatural sign at just the precise moment "closed the sale" to put it in salesman's terms. There was no longer any room for doubt in their minds. He was the Son of God.

RESURRECTION APPEARANCES RESCUE FOLLOWERS' FLOUNDERING FAITH

The disciples, like the Old Testament Israelites, (and 21st century Christians) had trouble maintaining their faith when they faced new challenges, even though God had proven Himself to them in so many awesome ways. But Jesus was gone from their physical sight and it seems that none of them actually expected Him to come back to life, even though He had repeatedly tried to tell them that He would.

Jesus first appeared to Mary Magdalene. She had brought spices and wanted to show respect to His body in the customary way. But His body was not there. Instead, the tomb was empty. Neither she nor the disciples saw the empty tomb as a positive sign. Rather, she was upset that someone had moved His body. How could she do what she had come to do?

When Jesus appeared to her, she did not even recognize Him when He first spoke to her. But **when He spoke her name**, she turned to Him and addressed Him as "Rabboni!" or "teacher!"

It was **when Jesus spoke her name** that she acknowledged Him for who He was. We find that people often respond the same to specific words from God. Often, they can hear a good message and not respond because they did not hear God speak their name. It was just a general truth being preached. In their pain, it did not penetrate their spirit.

But when they hear a specific word addressed to them from the Lord, who knows the secret pain and fears of their heart, they begin to cry out and address Him as Savior and Lord. We have seen so many examples of this in our own prophetic ministry. My wife, Brenda, has a special gift of bringing people to faith in this manner. In effect people respond like Mary, saying, **"He knows my name. It must be Jesus."**

Next Jesus appeared to ten of His disciples. Judas had hanged himself and Thomas, the notorious skeptic, was absent at the time. The disciples had doubted the enthusiastic Mary Magdalene, but had gathered together for fear of the Jews.

Jesus appeared to them, spoke peace to them and showed them His scars. John reports that they were glad when they saw Him. (John 20:20)

But Thomas would not believe any reports and protested that he would have to see and touch the scars himself before he would believe. Some have speculated that Thomas had earlier been fooled many times because of his innocent faith. Now he wouldn't believe anyone until he had personal evidence.

At any rate, when Jesus appeared to all the disciples a week later, Thomas was present and Jesus approached him to show him His wounds, inviting him to put his fingers on them. Notice the dialogue in the following two verses:

"And Thomas answered and said to Him, 'My Lord and my God!' Jesus said to him, 'Thomas, because you have seen Me, you have believed. Blessed are those who have not seen and yet have believed.'" (John 20:28,29)

Here we find Jesus acknowledging the fact that a physical manifestation or sign has helped Thomas believe. But Jesus pronounced a special blessing on those who would believe without such a physical manifestation.

My personal conviction is that He is saying that some have exercised their spiritual senses to know Him through intimacy of their spirit with His. They are the ones who are truly blessed, because they know Him on a deeper level. Also their faith is more solid, because it is based on a relationship that cannot be shaken by changes in the physical environment.

Those who see Jesus and hear His voice with spiritual senses become less and less dependent on their physical senses to live the Christian life. They develop a strong trust that takes them through life's greatest storms. They are constantly experiencing signs and wonders that are of a spiritual nature. Some of them see visions and angels. Some hear God's still small voice and receive fresh revelations from the throne room. They all experience the presence of God in various and awesome ways and no one can tell them that God is not real.

But they still cry out for God to do the physical signs and wonders, because they so want others to know God as they do. And before unbelievers can get to know Him, they must believe that He exists, and most of the time, they need a little boost to get started in a life of faith.

JOHN'S CONCLUSION: SIGNS PRODUCE BELIEF

Before we move on to the early church record, one more Scripture in John is very significant to our study. The last two verses of John 20 sum up his purpose for writing about the signs which Jesus did.

*"And truly Jesus did many other **signs** in the presence of His disciples, which are not written in this book; but **these are written that you may believe that Jesus is the Christ, the Son of God, and that believing you may have life in His name."'* (John 20:30,31)

The gospel of John has been called "The Gospel of Belief". None of the other gospels focus on belief as John does. The famous verse, John 3:16 is the classic "good news" verse that says that if we believe we have everlasting life.

In these important verses, quoted above, that reveal his purpose for writing, John makes it very clear that He is writing about the signs that Jesus did so that his readers would believe in Jesus and receive everlasting life. John was writing for those who would have their spirits open to someone who was anointed to preach the Word of God, and who was giving honest testimonies of what they had seen.

Of course, we know that there are those who believe the stories of others, but there are others like Thomas, who need to see for themselves. For them, telling the stories will not be enough. They need to see the signs and wonders with their own eyes before they will believe.

Should we say that these people don't deserve to be Christians, because they won't believe the testimony of someone else? Jesus told people if they didn't believe His own words that they should believe in the works, or signs, which He did. His heart was to bring them all to faith in His name.

John, who leaned on Jesus' breast, had the same heart beat as Jesus. He also had a passion to make it as easy as possible for people to believe. He knew that the more signs he reported, the easier it would be for some to believe. Therefore, he wrote about the signs the way he did.

John, himself had been part of a powerful miracle-working church, as recorded in the book of Acts. We will be moving on to that account shortly. Before we do that, we should look into one other aspect of belief in the gospels, which actually anticipated personal miracles.

JESUS PRAISES FAITH IN OTHERS

There are numerous stories of miracles, which took place in Jesus' ministry, where we read that Jesus complimented the great faith of those who sought Him for healing. These included the woman with the issue of blood, who reached out to touch Jesus' garment, and the Roman centurion, who said, "Just speak the word and my servant will be healed." Other examples were the persistent blind man, who wouldn't be quiet, and the equally-persistent woman from Canaan, who had a severely demon-possessed daughter.

There were also many others to whom He said, "Your faith has made you whole." We will not look at all these stories individually, but we want to try to understand where this strong faith came from.

Scripture does not seem to give us too many clues as to the source of their special faith, but if we understand the principles, which have already been discovered in our research, we can probably get a pretty good idea of what Jesus was talking about.

First of all, they all had great needs, and they had no one else to go to. The woman with the issue of blood had spent everything she had on fruitless treatments and had no other hope left but Jesus.

The blind men were in a similar situation, with no natural means of sight. The Canaanite mother and the centurion could not buy from anyone the miracles that they were desperate for. They knew they needed a supernatural power.

Doubtless, they had all heard the stories circulating about Jesus of Nazareth. In their broken and contrite hearts, they had cried out to their Heavenly Father for mercy. Their spiritual senses had become active in their communication with God, their only hope. God gave grace to the humble, even as He resisted the proud Pharisees.

These desperate folks received a revelation of God in their spirit that said, "If you can present yourself before Jesus, He will have mercy on you." Each of them had a passion to see Him or touch Him. They pressed in because they already had a revelation from God that He was their healer.

The centurion knew that Jesus was the Son of God, under the authority of His Father, God. He knew this by revelation. Jesus saw this as greater faith than He had seen in all of Israel.

Personally, I can say that the most difficult or impossible situations in my own life have resulted in greater faith than all the blessings I have ever received. The reason, of course, is that when my back was against the wall, I cried out to God and took time to listen to what He had to say back to me. The result was a new level of intimacy in the spirit realm.

We don't look forward to tests and trials, but when they come, we can look upon them as blessings in disguise, because they can build our faith, which is more valuable than perishable gold. (I Peter 1:7)

CHAPTER 9

Early Church Explodes With Signs and Converts

After Jesus ascended to Heaven, He sent the same Holy Spirit, who had inhabited His own body on the earth, to His waiting disciples. Inhabited by the same Holy Spirit as Jesus was, His new body had the same power as Jesus possessed, when He walked the shores of Galilee and the hills of Judea.

THE POWER OF UNITY TO PRODUCE SIGNS

The Holy Spirit did not fall upon a group of self-centered individuals, who were still arguing about who would be the greatest in the Kingdom of Jesus. Rather, Luke makes it very clear in Acts 1 and 2 that the 120 in the upper room were all in one accord in one place for ten days.

The Holy Spirit fell on a united body which was totally obedient to one head, and all the members of the body were in loving relationship with the others. This enabled the church to demonstrate the same power that Jesus demonstrated, and the results were similar to the results that Jesus had. You can read a clear presentation of this concept in my earlier book, *"Heal Your Body, Lord."* It includes much of my testimony and how God gave me this revelation during a personal revival in my youth.

My personal conviction is that the unity of the disciples in the upper room emanated from the brokenness they experienced following their total failure at the cross. That brokenness, followed by Jesus' forgiveness, combined with a deep feeling of emptiness and desperation when Jesus departed, changed their hearts forever.

They had all been forgiven much and therefore they all loved much. They were now willing to die for Jesus, if given the chance, and most of them eventually were. They wanted nothing but to please Jesus, who had done so much for them, and to prosper His Kingdom.

SIGNS AND WONDERS BEGIN

When the day of Pentecost had come, the Holy Spirit swept down upon them as a rushing mighty wind. This was accompanied by tongues of fire that fell on each one. Then their own tongues became instruments of the Holy Spirit to speak the "wonderful works of God" in the unlearned foreign languages of those around them.

FIRST SIGN – RUSHING MIGHTY WIND

Each of these individual signs had a message that God wanted to speak to the people of Jerusalem. The first sign, the sound of a mighty rushing wind, spoke to them of an invisible but awesome power that was about to move things around and upset the old apple cart of religion for everyone.

The Greek words for spirit, breath and wind all have the same root. The wind of the Spirit of God was blowing the breath of life into the waiting disciples. The disciples received the life-giving oxygen of the Holy Spirit's breath and they were filled with an invisible but very real and dynamic power.

SECOND SIGN – CLOVEN TONGUES AS OF FIRE

The second sign of the "cloven tongues as of fire" carried with it a message that God was setting each one of them on fire with a passion for His Kingdom. They were being given the power (dunamis) of the Holy Spirit. Fire was one of the most powerful entities known to man at that time. Thus it represented power as well as passion.

All of the 120 experienced the same wind, but each one had his individual flame of fire. We all feel the breath of the same Spirit, but

He manifests through us in an individual way. This is a picture of **unity with individuality,** which is found throughout the Scripture, especially in the teachings of Paul about the body of Jesus.

THIRD SIGN – SPEAKING UNLEARNED LANGUAGES

The third sign of speaking in foreign tongues carried many individual messages to many foreigners, but the general message was two-fold. **First of all, it said that the anointing to witness is for everyone who receives Jesus and His Holy Spirit.** Jesus promised that when the Holy Spirit came upon the disciples that they would be witness unto him. (Acts 1:8)

Peter was clearly the spiritual leader, but he did not do all the ministering. Each one of the 120 were speaking to individuals about the awesome things of God. No one was left in a corner thinking they had nothing to offer because they were not gifted like others.

The second message of this third sign was that God cares about each unbelieving individual that we find in our environment, and He tailors words of grace and truth just for them. I believe God wants each lost soul that we encounter to receive a specific word of love and mercy that has their name on it. Even as Jesus spoke Mary Magdalene's name, and she responded with worship, He wants to speak the name of everyone who needs an encounter with Him.

That is why Paul told us to desire earnestly to prophesy, because prophecy is the main tool God uses to speak someone's name to get their attention so He can reveal His love to them. We have seen God do this in our own ministry so many times. Both Christians and non-Christians need to hear God speak their names. The greatest joy in ministry is seeing people being transformed from an attitude of fear and hopelessness to an attitude of faith and excitement by the power of God to reveal that He knows their name.

For those who desire to understand more about the biblical use of prophetic ministry, I would recommend our earlier book, *"The Dynamics of Biblical Prophetic Ministry"*. The book discusses many

SIGNS AND WONDERS: TO SEEK OR NOT TO SEEK

very important, but often ignored Scripture passages that teach us the importance of the proper use of the prophetic gift.

POWER AND CONTENT OF PETER'S MESSAGE

When the crowds quickly gathered, the preaching anointing fell on Peter. He used the attention-gathering power of the signs and wonders to kick off a powerful and spontaneous message.

Peter's message focuses almost exclusively on the supernatural. He quotes three prophecies from the Old Testament. The first is from Joel. Peter refers to the last days' prophecy of God's Spirit being poured out on all flesh. Not only would there be prophecies, visions and dreams, but there would be:

"... wonders in heaven above, and signs in the earth beneath." *(Acts 2:19)*

Peter then makes the following declaration about Jesus,

"Men of Israel, hear these words: Jesus of Nazareth, a Man attested by God to you by miracles, wonders and signs, which God did through Him in your midst, as you yourselves also know." (Acts 2:22)

The point is that Peter made it clear that God wanted to help people believe in His Son. The miracles, wonders and signs were not only to bless individuals that had needs. They were also to attest that Jesus was the Son of God. The signs had a message. At the end of the message Peter was interrupted by the cries from the crowd:

"Men and brethren, what shall we do?" *(Acts 2:37)*

Peter declared that they should repent and be baptized, and that they would receive the gift of the Holy Ghost. After exhorting them with many other words, we read that about three thousand souls were added to them.

The excitement created by the explosion of signs and wonders spread quickly to the new converts. Luke reports that:

". . . they continued steadfastly in the apostles' doctrine and fellowship, in the breaking of bread and in prayers. Then fear came upon every soul, and many **wonders and signs** were done through the apostles. (Acts 2:42)

Luke goes on to tell us that the whole church was in great unity and the people spent much time together in fellowship. Many people sold possessions and shared with those who had needs. The excitement was so high that the people couldn't get enough of this new thing called "church". Read carefully the following:

"So continuing daily with one accord in the temple, and breaking bread from house to house, they ate their food with gladness and simplicity of heart, praising God and having favor with all the people. And the Lord added to the church daily those who were being saved." (Acts 2:46, 47)

Every day they had church, and every day people were being saved and added to their numbers. The Jews and others in Jerusalem in those days had never seen anything like it. They had been religious and reverend and pious, but they had never heard of having joy and excitement in their religion. This was a whole new concept and the common folk loved it. Of course, the religious crowd had a different reaction.

MIRACLES BRING EXCITEMENT AND JOY

How well I remember those exciting six weeks in Argentina in the fall of 1973. Churches had been struggling with many issues. Pastors had not been talking to other pastors in their city. But when God began to do some powerful miracles through my friend and mentor, E. R. Burnette, everything changed.

Almost immediately pastors were being reconciled to each other and began to work together to support the meetings. The Spirit of joy and love was flowing like a mighty river. The excitement just continued to grow as night after night more wonderful miracles occurred. We had meetings, usually two a day, for three and one half weeks before we took a day or two of rest. The miracles kept people coming night after night and bringing more people with them.

And every night after a number of visible miracles and amazing testimonies, people would accept Jesus for the first time, until the numbers added up to about one thousand. Every day people were being added to the church, for the same reason they were added to the church in the book of Acts. When people saw something that was more exciting than religion, it was like they had just fallen in love with Jesus. They just couldn't get enough of Jesus, and they couldn't get enough fellowship with the people He was working through.

We know God is at work in His church when people want to be at church every day. When they come expecting the unexpected on a regular basis, the Spirit of the Lord is probably in reality the special speaker. And when many of them are bringing their unsaved friends, who become believers in large numbers, then more than likely, special miracles, signs and wonders are taking place.

ONE LAME MAN A'LEAPING

When Peter and John headed for the temple at the hour of prayer, they encountered the lame beggar who was born lame and was now over 40 years old. When the man who had never walked in his life began "walking and leaping and praising God", there was another instant gathering of a great crowd at Solomon's Porch of the temple. Notice the following narrative:

*"and they were filled with **wonder** and amazement at what had happened to him. Now as the lame man who was healed held on to Peter and John, all the people **ran** together to them in the porch which is called Solomon's, **greatly amazed.**" (Acts 3:11)*

This wonder caused people to run towards the apostles. No one had to beg people to come to a crusade; they weren't advertising on television; they weren't doing any of the things we might do to promote a meeting; but the people ran towards them to find out what all the excitement was about.

Excitement is always a major player in a revival or a move of God. People can't stop talking about what God is doing, and people can't stay away for fear they will miss some more excitement. God has equipped the church with signs and wonders to keep the element of excitement in the church, so that people will again run to the meeting place to find out "what's happenin'?"

PETER'S SECOND SPONTANEOUS MESSAGE

Again Peter, under a strong preaching anointing, stirred the hearts of the crowd with his description of Jesus. In this eleven-verse message he referred to prophets six times and quotes several prophetic verses from the Old Testament.

The end result was two-fold. First of all we read that the religious leaders were "greatly disturbed" and had the apostles arrested. The second result was as follows:

"However, many of those who heard the word believed; and the number of the men came to be about five thousand." (Acts 4:4)

The church saw explosive growth in numbers on the same level as the explosion of signs and wonders. This growth was not just a temporary "flash in the pan" kind of growth. These people were planted into the daily fellowship and teachings of the church. Later in this chapter we read:

"Now the multitude of those who believed were of one heart and one soul:" (Acts 4:32)

Please note that it wasn't just the 12 or the 120 that were in one accord, but now it was the whole multitude of believers. The scripture goes on to reveal that they were extremely unselfish and continued to sell property and possessions for the sake of the Kingdom of God.

BOLDNESS OF WITNESS AMAZES RELIGIOUS LEADERS

When the Sanhedrin began to interrogate the apostles, the Spirit of God came on Peter again with great boldness. In response to a question about how or by what power the lame man was healed, Peter threw all caution to the wind and blasted them with both barrels.

He courageously proclaimed the power and authority of the name of Jesus, saying that all men must call on His name in order to be saved. He then boldly charged them with murdering the long-awaited Messiah. Let's listen in to a part of Peter's anointed verbal barrage:

> *"let it be known to you all, and to all the people of Israel, that by the name of Jesus Christ of Nazareth, **whom you crucified, whom God raised from the dead**, by Him this man stands here before you whole. This was the stone which was rejected by you builders, which has become the chief cornerstone. Nor is there salvation in any other, for there is no other name under heaven given among men by which we must be saved." (Acts 4:10-12)*

Notice the highlighted phrases. Peter is clearly stating that the Sanhedrin was in direct opposition to God. He is making them the enemies of God, which of course would be very infuriating to them. But the boldness of Peter caught them rather by surprise. Jesus had ended his public ministry as a Lamb who opened not His mouth to defend Himself. But Peter, who had earlier denied even knowing Jesus, was now roaring like a lion in defense of His Savior. This "anointed boldness" was a wonder to the Sanhedrin. Luke comments:

> *"Now when they say the boldness of Peter and John, and perceived that they were uneducated and untrained men, **they marveled**. And they realized that they had been with Jesus." (Acts 4:13)*

Jesus had been with His Father and did the works of His Father. Peter and John had been with Jesus and did the works of Jesus. They had been with Jesus in the natural, but they had since been with Jesus in Spirit. The same Holy Spirit, who inhabited the Christ, now was inhabiting them. The same methods that Jesus used to make people marvel, were now being used by His disciples.

The boldness of Peter and John left the Sanhedrin virtually speechless. They ordered them out of the hearing room and admitted they couldn't argue with the fact that a great miracle had been done. They decided to threaten them and let them go, for fear of the people.

When they had issued their stern threats not to mention the name of Jesus, Peter and John responded with more courageous words of defiance:

"Whether it is right in the sight of God to listen to you more than to God, you judge. For we cannot but speak the things which we have seen and heard." (Acts 4:19, 20)

Of course, the beginning of persecution kept the level of excitement in the church high. The response of the church was to have a powerful prayer meeting. This passage was referred to early in the book. **We find the church praying that healings, signs and wonders would be done in the name of Jesus. The purpose for these was increased boldness to preach the name of Jesus.**

God responded with a fresh outpouring of the Holy Spirit, accompanied by a shaking of the place they were in. The disciples responded by speaking "the word of God with boldness." Luke adds:

"And with great power the apostles gave witness to the resurrection of the Lord Jesus. And great grace was upon them all." (Acts 4:33)

The word "power" used above is the Greek word "dunamis", which is sometimes translated miracle. And so the cycle continues:

- Signs and wonders produce curiosity.
- Curiosity attracts a crowd.
- The gospel is preached.
- People believe and are converted.
- Fresh faith of new converts produces more signs and wonders.

DIVINE JUDGMENT KEEPS CHURCH PURE: DECEITFUL DUO DROP DEAD

Opposition to revival will always come from two sources: without and within. The persecution from the Jewish leaders could not stop the progress of the exploding church. The enemy of the church then tried to corrupt the church from within. Although he was much more successful with this technique later on in history, the first attempt at polluting the purity and unity of the early church was stopped in its tracks, through the power of the Holy Spirit gift of discerning of spirits.

Ananias and Sapphira brought the first sin into the camp. This was similar to what happened when the Children of Israel entered the "promised land" and Achan hid some contraband in his tent. Both of these cases were dealt with in a similar way. The wages of sin is death and God was illustrating this truth.

I believe that God was demonstrating what would happen if sin was allowed in the camp. Neither in the Old Testament nor in the New do we find this kind of judgment repeated. But God was saying that His church would suffer spiritual death, if they let sin destroy their pure love for Jesus.

The church, like the Children of Israel, fell from its place and position of power, and was conquered by its enemy and brought into bondage. This happened gradually as the church grew in numbers and incorporated many people and nations into Christianity. The end result was a powerless church in the dark ages.

Just as natural Israel lost her possessions (her land), when she was conquered by Assyria and Babylon, so spiritual Israel (the Church of Jesus) lost her possessions (supernatural power and spiritual gifts) as sin infiltrated the people of God, bringing division and strife. But just as natural Israel has been restored to her possessions, even so spiritual Israel has been recovering her divine possessions.

RESULTS OF DIVINE JUSTICE

The immediate response of the people who saw or heard about the sudden deaths of the deceitful duo was as follows:

*"So **great fear** came upon all the church and upon all who heard these things." (Acts 5:11)*

The next result mentioned was another great demonstration of the supernatural power of God. This was followed by another declaration of the unity of the body of Jesus, which was followed by another statement of the respect and fear the people felt toward the church. Please read the narrative given by Luke:

*"And through the hands of the apostles **many signs and wonders** were done among the people. And **they were all with one
accord** in Solomon's Porch. Yet none of the rest dared join them,
but the people esteemed them highly." (Acts 5:12,13)*

But the following verse gives us the result that we are looking for in this study:

*"**And believers were increasingly added to the Lord, multitudes
of both men and women,"** (Acts 5: 14)*

- The miracle of divine justice, produced a respect among the people.
- The atmosphere of faith created was conducive to more signs and wonders.
- The signs and wonders resulted from and reproduced more unity.
- The signs and wonders coupled with the unity and respect of the people, produced multitudes of believers, both men and women.

INCREDIBLE CLIMAX TO PREVIOUS EVENTS

The last verse quoted, which described the great harvest of believers, ended with a comma rather than a period. Luke wasn't finished describing the amazing consequences of the Holy Spirit's execution of divine justice on the "deceitful duo". He goes on to describe an amazing healing and deliverance event, which has probably never been equaled since that day. Read the following with both eyes and ears open:

*"so that they brought the sick out into the streets and laid them
on beds and couches, that at least the shadow of Peter passing by
might fall on some of them. Also a multitude gathered from the*

*surrounding cities to Jerusalem, bringing sick people and those who were tormented by unclean spirits, and **they were all healed.**" (Acts 5:15,16)*

- The results of one sign and wonder produced many signs and wonders. (Luke 5:12)
- Many signs and wonders produced many believers. (Luke 5:14)
- The believers' belief, or faith, reproduced the powerful healing and deliverance event we just quoted.

In this glorious expression of the power of unity and faith, we read that not one person who was afflicted with demons or disease left the way they had come. And we are told that there were multitudes from both Jerusalem and all the surrounding cities. There were so many that their only hope of getting touched by Peter was getting touched by his shadow.

But the faith of the people was so stimulated by the events which had taken place that it drew out the power of God from the presence of God emanating from Peter. **Here we find that not only do miracles produce believers, but the new believers produce more miracles.**

This, of course, is what Jesus promised in His farewell talk with His disciples:

*"**And these signs shall follow those who believe**: In My name they will cast out demons; they will speak with new tongues; they will take up serpents; and if they drink anything deadly, it will by no means hurt them; they will lay hands on the sick, and they will recover." (Mark 16:17,18)*

Believers who come to faith as a result of seeing God's power, will naturally have more faith for more signs and wonders. Their fresh faith draws out the power and anointing that is on apostolic and prophetic leaders in the church. The result is more signs and wonders to create more faith in others.

DEACONS CHOSEN – GOSPEL SPREADS

Along with converts, the healing crusade produced a fresh onslaught of persecution. Arrested again, the apostles repeated their bold accusation that their persecutors had murdered the "Prince and Savior" of the Jews. This time the apostles were not only threatened, they were also beaten, which was a very painful experience to endure.

But they came back with great joy that they were counted worthy to suffer for the name of Jesus. This level of faith and love for Jesus had come as a result of a process of brokenness, forgiveness and the outpouring of the Holy Spirit's power. The many signs and wonders provided constant reassurance that God was with them.

In the sixth chapter of Acts, the second recorded church problem occurred. The Greek-speaking, or Hellenist Jews began to murmur against the Hebrew Jews, that their widows were being neglected in the daily distribution.

Notice that no extreme judgment took place, as in the case of Ananias and Saphira. Instead, the apostles decided to administrate the problem by choosing seven deacons, who would see to it that everyone was treated fairly. This was not only the second problem for the church, but the first real expression of disunity, which would eventually diminish the flow of supernatural power in the church.

But the apostles made the best of the situation by delegating ministry to seven others who were chosen for their good reputation and the fact that they were "full of the Holy Spirit and wisdom." They chose Stephen, a man "full of faith and the Holy Spirit", and six other notable Christian leaders, who received the ministry of the laying on of the hands of the apostles.

The next comment made by Luke after reporting the above process is the following:

*"And the word of God spread, and **the number of the disciples multiplied greatly** in Jerusalem, and a great many of the priests were obedient to the faith. And Stephen, full of faith and power, did great **wonders and signs** among the people." (Acts 6:7,8)*

Notice the highlighted words above. The fact that the disciples were being multiplied is reported before the fact that Stephen was doing the wonders and signs. As we pointed out previously, the normal order is for the signs to precede the conversions, but again, as we just observed, the new believers and the expansion and enthusiasm of a tremendously excited church just kept producing more and more supernatural results.

Another note-worthy point is that when the church produced the signs and wonders, there was a major polarization occurring in those who observed. Those who were open to truth responded positively, but those who were opposed to anything that could dethrone them from their position of power, reacted in a strongly negative way.

All of a sudden, the religious leaders not only had twelve apostles to deal with, but now they had seven deacons as well. At least two of these (but more than likely all of them) were making the same kind of problems for them that the twelve had been making.

Their reaction to this problem was swift and violent. Using false witnesses, they did the same thing to Stephen as they did to Jesus, accusing him of blaspheming God. As they stoned him, he had an open vision of Heaven with Jesus standing at the right hand of God. While his face shone like an angel's, he asked God not to charge them with the sin they were committing.

One of the men watching him die and giving his approval was Saul of Tarsus, later to become the apostle Paul. Perhaps Stephen's call for forgiveness had something to do with God's mercy regarding Paul. At any rate, the vision of Stephen dying surely must have made a life-long impression on the young Jewish zealot.

SAMARATIANS SEE SIGNS AND BELIEVE

Following Stephen's death as the first Christian martyr, great persecution occurred against the church, resulting in the scattering of the church throughout Judea and Samaria. The apostles, however, remained in Jerusalem.

Philip, the second deacon mentioned in Acts 6, went to Samaria and preached the gospel to the Samaritans. Notice the following quote, which clearly reinforces the point we have been consistently making in this study.

*"And the multitudes with one accord heeded the things spoken by Philip, **hearing and seeing the miracles** which he did. For unclean spirits, crying with a loud voice, came out of many who were possessed; and many who were paralyzed and lame were healed. And there was great joy in that city." (Acts 8:6-8)*

The church had silenced Stephen, but now Philip, the second deacon, was reaching multitudes in Samaria, using the same strategy that was used by the Holy Spirit through the apostles. God gave the people something to see to go along with what they heard to make the argument much more convincing.

We have always heard that we remember much more of what we see than what we hear. I guess God must have heard about that too, because He has been incorporating that knowledge into His strategy for many millennia.nd when we see something that sticks in our minds, we more easily remember what we heard when it happened.

Notice another great truth revealed in this story. The people not only believed, but because of all the great things that were happening to them and their friends and family, they were full of joy. We are told that "The joy of the Lord is our strength." (Nehemiah 8:10) If this is true, then **one powerful result of signs and wonders is that our strength increases.**

No wonder our enemy wants us not to push for signs and wonders. He knows that without them the church will not be as full of the joy of the Lord and we will not have as much strength to fight against him.

I personally have seen this principle at work over and over again. Whether it is a proliferation of signs and wonders and miraculous healings, such as I saw in Argentina in 1973, or a number of prophetic words of encouragement that involve supernatural words of knowledge, the result is the same. People are filled with joy and they gain strength to walk with the Lord. We could give a multitude of real-life illustrations to verify this truth, but we will restrain ourselves at this point for the sake of brevity.

SIMON THE SORCERER OVERPOWERED

When the Harry Potter movie hit the theaters with an incredible reception from the American public, I wrote a message to those on our e-mail mailing list. I stated that the church needed to do a better job to demonstrate the superior power of the Holy Spirit.

I further mentioned that I would love to see a high quality movie about the power of the early church, where so many times the power of the Holy Spirit is shown to overpower the comparatively weak strength of our enemy. One of these examples would be the story of Simon, the sorcerer, from Acts 8.

Simon was one of those in Samaria who saw the miracles performed through the ministry of Philip. Up to that time, he had been the "Big Dog" in the community. Luke declares:

"But there was a certain man called Simon, who previously practiced sorcery in the city and astonished the people of Samaria, claiming that he was someone great, to whom they all gave heed, from the least to the greatest, saying, 'This man is the great power of God.' And they heeded him because he had astonished them with his sorceries for a long time." (Acts 8:9-11)

Again we see that people believed when they saw the supernatural, even when it came from the devil. Some may think that things like this do not happen in our sophisticated, scientific society. But if that is truly the case, then why are the psychics such a success on television, and why is Harry Potter such a phenomenon? And why do so many people consult their horoscopes, etc.?

But Simon, who saw a power far greater than his own, himself believed as Luke describes:

*"Then Simon himself also believed; and when he was baptized he continued with Philip, and was amazed, **seeing the miracles and signs** which were done." (Acts 8:13)*

Simon continued to be amazed at the power of God, but being accustomed to being in the spotlight, he thought that perhaps he could get back some of the attention to himself. When the apostles, Peter and John came down to lay hands on the new Christians and pray for them to receive the Holy Spirit, Simon offered to pay them money to have the same power. Obviously, when they received the Holy Spirit something observable took place. Many speculate that they also spoke in tongues, but that is, of course, only undocumented speculation.

Peter, operating in his prophetic gifting, rebuked him sharply and warned him to repent. He revealed to Simon that he had been **"poisoned by bitterness and bound by iniquity."** (Acts 8:23) Simon humbled himself again and asked Peter to pray for him.

LESSONS LEARNED FROM SIMON'S STORY

1. Believers still have problems.

Simon's story reveals the truth that a person can be a genuine believer and baptized by a genuine man of God, and yet still be in bondage to various things. Satan obviously had a hold in Simon's life through things that had happened in his past. Bitterness comes from negative experiences that were not handled in a proper manner. The result was iniquity. The Greek word used here for iniquity is "adikia", meaning (legal) injustice.

Simon needed to deal with his past sins and hurts and repent so that God could take away the injustice that had been his mode of operation as a sorcerer. He wanted power again so he could get people's praise and respect. But he would use the power in an unjust manner, probably getting more wealth through this power. That would explain the fact that he was offering money. We usually invest money to make more money. And of course, the bitterness that he had not yet dealt with would make him feel justified in doing what was unjust in God's sight.

2. We need all the gifts working together.

We see the need here for the different ministries that God has given to the church. Philip was an evangelist, as well as a deacon. Like many evangelists, his gifts were in the area of the miraculous. Many were healed and delivered under his ministry. Then he baptized all who believed, thus asking them for a strong commitment to Jesus.

But Philip never led them into receiving the Holy Spirit in the way that he had received Him. Peter and John came up to Samaria to help them receive the Holy Spirit. And Philip, who had cast out many demons, had not discerned the bitterness and iniquity in Simon. It took the prophetic gift of discerning of spirits in Peter to expose that need in Simon's life.

PHILIP GOES ON A SPECIAL ASSIGNMENT

After Peter and John had ministered in many Samaritan villages, Philip was visited by an angel, who told him to leave the revival meetings in Samaria and head south on the road which goes from Jerusalem to Gaza. This is the desert area known as the Gaza Strip. Philip obeyed the angel and found himself behind a man in a chariot, who is known to us as "the Ethiopian Eunuch". This man was a high ranking Ethiopian government official, the treasurer for Queen Candace.

Although it was a desert area and likely very hot, the Holy Spirit told Philip to overtake the chariot. We are told that Philip ran to catch up with him. While overtaking the chariot, Philip heard the man reading Isaiah, the prophet.

The eunuch was returning from Jerusalem, where he had gone to worship and was struggling with a clear messianic prophecy. Philip offered his help and began to explain Jesus to him. The eunuch believed and was baptized. After the baptism, Philip was super-naturally transported away and was found at Azotus, or Ashdod, a city north of Gaza along the Mediterranean Sea.

From the information we are given in the story, we have no evidence that the Ethiopian eunuch saw any miracle or supernatural sign and wonder to bring him to faith in Jesus. But the story begins with an angelic appearance and ends with a rare miracle – the miraculous transportation of Philip from one place to another.

When Philip preached to him, he no doubt told him the story of the angelic message he had received. And when he preached Jesus to him, he of course told him of the supernatural resurrection of Jesus, as well as the many miracles He had done in the sight of His disciples.

Another possibility of the supernatural is in the instructions given to Philip by the angel. The word translated, "south" in this story could also be translated "mid-day" or "noon". Its basic meaning in the Greek is "middle of the day." If this is what was conveyed to Philip, then he was given a scheduled appointment by the angel.

The fact that Philip was there just when the eunoch needed someone to explain Isaiah to him and the fact that an angel had sent Philip, was enough of the miraculous to convince the eunuch, if he needed any convincing by then. When Philip miraculously disappeared from his sight, he had more proof that his faith in Philip's message was justified and he went on his way with confidence and a changed heart.

SAUL SEES LIGHT, GOES BLIND, BELIEVES

The next notable convert to Christianity recorded by Luke was the Apostle Paul, know earlier as Saul of Tarsus. Although Saul had been very zealous to try to stamp out the Christian faith, approving of Stephen's stoning, God had mercy on him and gave him a special divine encounter on the Damascus road.

Saul had undoubtedly heard of the miraculous signs and wonders that had been performed through the church. He may even have seen some of them. But Saul was a hardened Pharisee and God knew what it would take to bring him to faith. Again we see the patience and mercy of God to help us to believe in Him.

God was, of course, having mercy on the church at the same time as He was having mercy on Saul. No one had caused more problems for them than Saul. God dealt Saul's plans and ambitions a crippling blow as He set an ambush for him on the Damascus road.

Saul saw a blinding light, which knocked him to the ground. Then he heard the voice of Jesus accusing Saul of persecuting Him. Saul arose from the encounter "trembling and astonished", as well as totally blind, and asked Jesus what he should do. Jesus told him to enter the city and wait for further instructions. Without food or drink for three days, Saul waited in the house of Judas for God to show him what to do.

Next God sent a man, named Ananias, to pray for Saul. God gave the reluctant prophet twelve specific bits of knowledge about Saul to give him the courage to go and minister to this much-feared enemy of the saints.

Saul was given back his sight, was filled with the Holy Spirit and was baptized. Remaining with the disciples in Damascus for a few days, he immediately began to preach Jesus in the synagogues, that He indeed was the Son of God. This amazed everyone who heard him (Acts 9:21). Then Luke adds:

"But Saul increased all the more in strength, and confounded the Jews who dwelt in Damascus, proving that this Jesus is the Christ." (Acts 9:22)

From later recorded witnessing sessions, we know that Paul usually shared his testimony of meeting Jesus on the road and being blinded by His glory. Using both his own testimony and the Old Testament prophecies, he was able to convince many to believe in Jesus.

Without his supernatural divine encounter, Saul, himself, would not have been convinced to believe in Jesus. And of course, he would not have convinced anyone else to believe in Jesus like he did in Damascus. Instead he would have continued his murderous ways, and would have never gone to the nations or written most of the New Testament. What a tragedy that would have been! It seems inconceivable to think of the early church without an Apostle Paul, or the Bible without Paul's epistles.

But because of one "Divine Supernatural Moment" in Saul's life, the course of history was dramatically changed and the Kingdom of God was powerfully enriched.

But even today, God is raising up powerful witnesses to His resurrection. Many saints have experienced His power in an awesome way and they joyfully and sincerely speak about it to many hungry people, who gladly receive the hope of eternal life.

After Saul's conversion many of the saints were still fearful of him, but finally, through Barnabas and others, he was accepted by all the brethren. At the same time, the non-Christian Jews began to plot to take his life, but God protected him. Luke adds this comment:

"Then the churches throughout all Judea, Galilee, and Samaria had peace and were edified. And walking in the fear of the Lord and in the comfort of the Holy Spirit, they were multiplied."
(Acts 9:31)

PARALYSIS HEALED – CITIES CONVERTED

Peter apparently was traveling throughout the land of Israel, visiting the saints wherever he went. When he came to Lydda, he found a man named Aeneas, "who had been bedridden eight years and was paralyzed. (Acts 9:33)

Peter spoke to him and proclaimed him healed. Aeneas responded by rising to his feet and revealing to all around the supernatural power of God. Not only those in Lydda, but also those in a nearby town of Sharon were touched by the miracle:

"So all who dwelt at Lydda and Sharon saw him and turned to the Lord." (Acts 9:35)

This is really an amazing statement, which declares that **two whole cities were witnesses to this miracle and that every resident turned to the Lord in faith.** Again we see the power of one strategic miracle performed by God at the right time and place to accomplish the most for His glory.

DORCAS RESURRECTED – MANY BELIEVE

While Peter was still in Lydda, a very special woman named Tabitha (translated Dorcas), died in a neighboring town of Joppa. The disciples in Joppa sent for Peter who came immediately.

Peter was shown the tunics and garments which Dorcas had made for the local widows while she was alive. But Peter put them all out of the room and spoke life into the dead body of Dorcas, telling her to rise. She opened her eyes and sat up. Peter then presented her alive to the saints. The next verse tells us:

"And it became known throughout all Joppa, and many believed on the Lord." (Acts 9:42)

Joppa was probably considerably larger than Lydda or Sharon. Thus when it says "many believed", the numbers may have been as great, or even greater than the combined cities of Lydda and Sharon, where they all turned to the Lord. The important point, which has been repeated so many times, is that the miracle helped the people to believe in Jesus, and that is the desired result.

FIRST GENTILES BELIEVE

Cornelius was a Roman centurion (captain of 100 men) from the "Italian Regiment". He was already a devout believer in God, but didn't know about Jesus. Luke describes him as:

"a devout man and one who feared God with all his household, who gave alms generously to the people, and prayed to God always." (Acts 10:2)

This zealous convert to Judaism was visited by an angel of God in a vision. He was told that his prayers and alms "had come up for a memorial before God." (Acts 10:3) He was instructed to send for Peter and was given specific information about where to find him.

Meanwhile, Peter was given a lesson in New Covenant "Theology of Equality". He saw a vision of unclean beasts and was told to "kill and eat." After the third time, Peter was still confused as to the meaning of the vision. But just then messengers from Cornelias arrived, inviting him to come to his house. Then Peter understood the vision and came.

The message Peter preached included the fact that because God was with Jesus, and filled Him with the Holy Spirit and power, He went about "doing good and healing all who were oppressed by the devil." (Acts 10:38) The apostles, who also "had been with Jesus," (Acts 4:13) were of course doing the same things that Jesus did. I believe that we also, when we have been with Jesus, especially corporately, will do the same things that Jesus did.

The result of all these events including Peter's message, (which was interrupted by an outpouring of the Holy Spirit) was that the whole household of this Italian Centurion believed in Jesus. They were individually filled with the Holy Spirit and began to speak in tongues and magnify God. Then they were baptized in the name of the Lord.

This story reveals the lengths that God will go to in order to coordinate supernatural events for the purpose of bringing someone to faith in Jesus. The supernatural signs that took place also gave Peter the support that convinced his fellow apostles and leaders that taking the gospel to the Gentiles was not his own idea, but God's.

I believe that if Peter had nothing more than a personal conviction that he should take the gospel to the Gentiles, the rest of the Jerusalem church would have given him a lot more opposition. The fact that he had received visions, angelic visitations, and the fact that the Holy Spirit had manifested His gifts made Peter's mission undeniably a "God thing", and no one could argue with it.

Confirmation of this is found in Acts 11:

"If therefore God gave them the same gift as He gave us when we believed on the Lord Jesus Christ, who was I that I could withstand God? When they heard these things they became silent; and they glorified God, saying, 'Then God has also granted to the Gentiles repentance to life.'" (Acts 11:17,18)

Thus we find that **the believers believed Peter's declaration because of the signs** that accompanied the preaching of the gospel to the Gentiles.

FAITH SPREADS TO ANTIOCH

Soon others were ministering to the Gentiles. In Antioch there were men from Cyprus and Cyrene, who preached Jesus to the Greeks there. Luke gives us the following comment:

"And the hand of the Lord was with them, and a great number believed and turned to the Lord." (Acts 11:21)

While we have no report of specific signs and wonders in this brief account, the word "hand" that is used also has the meaning of "power". Thus we could translate the verse like this: "And the "power" of the Lord was with them". This could mean a strong anointing on the preaching, or it could mean that unreported signs and wonders took place.

When the leaders in Jerusalem heard the news, they sent Barnabas, who encouraged them to keep the faith. Luke declares:

"For he was a good man, full of the Holy Spirit and faith. And a great many people were added to the Lord." (Acts 11:24)

The description of Barnabas is almost identical to the description of Stephen, which we quoted earlier. The fact that Barnabas was full of the Holy Spirit and faith indicates to me that the Holy Spirit was manifesting through his life in some supernatural way. This of course includes producing lives that are transformed as well as bodies that are healed, etc. It goes without saying that a transformed life is the greatest miracle of all, but what we are learning is that more lives are transformed when they see a physical sign to reveal the love and power of God than when they don't.

CHAPTER 10

Paul and Company Reveal God's Power

PAUL AND BARNABAS HEAR THE CALL

In the Antioch church there were certain named prophets and teach ers. (Acts 13:1) As they ministered to the Lord and fasted, the Holy Spirit spoke, probably through one of the prophets, and directed them to send Barnabas and Saul into the ministry to which God was calling them. In response to this supernatural guidance, they laid hands on them and sent them away.

While no one was converted to Christianity at the time of this prophetic event, who could estimate how many became believers as a result of it? The impact on the history of the church and the whole world was huge. The book of Acts gives us a few highlights, which we will examine, but we know that we will only see the very tip of the tip of the proverbial iceberg.

PAUL DEFINES FULLY PREACHING THE GOSPEL

Before we examine the cases of conversions in Paul's ministry, let's hear what he has to say about it.

*"For I will not dare to speak of any of those things which Christ has not accomplished through me, **in word and deed, to make the Gentiles obedient – in mighty signs and wonders, by the power of the Spirit of God, so that from Jerusalem and round***

about to Illyricum I have fully preached the gospel of Christ."
(Romans 15:18,19)

First notice the expression **"in word and deed"**. This is the pattern we have seen so many times in our research. The **word** accompanied by the **deed** usually accomplishes much more than the word without the deed.

Now notice what was accomplished by the "word" and the "deed". The goal was to make the Gentiles obedient – or in other words, to bring them to faith and discipleship. **His goal was accomplished through the combination of word and deed**. If that was Paul's method, perhaps we should try to emulate him and seek to make it our method as well.

The next phrase removes all doubts as to what Paul meant by the word "deed". He described the deeds as **"mighty signs and wonders"**. Several of these are recorded in the book of Acts, but we can assume from Paul's statement that most of them were never recorded in Scripture.

Support for this conclusion comes from the next phrase, "so that **from Jerusalem and round about to Illyricum"**. The province of Illyricum was beyond Greece and near Italy. The area in between Illyricum and Jerusalem was Paul's evangelistic domain. He is plainly declaring that these "mighty signs and wonders" were done in all the areas in which he ministered.

So as we look at the ministry of Paul in various places, we will see that there are times when no miracles or signs are mentioned. We want to keep in mind that although we don't have specific miracles recorded in each place, we do have Paul's testimony in Romans that God did use him to show His miracle power everywhere he preached.

The final phrase, **"I have fully preached the gospel of Christ."** clearly reveals Paul's belief that **to fully preach the gospel, you need to demonstrate God's power and not just talk about it.**

This scripture is undoubtedly the source of the term, "Full Gospel", a common designation for churches who believe that God still performs the miraculous. It is a general term applied to Pentecostals and Charismatics and anyone who believes in preaching the supernatural.

Let me be a little picky here. Paul was not talking about a "Full Gospel"; he was talking about "fully preaching" the gospel. That means not having the right theology, but actually demonstrating it with signs and wonders. My concern about this term, which I, and many personal friends, have also used frequently, is that we might come across that we have it all together and others who believe differently don't. This term was chosen for some Pentecostal or Charismatic churches when there was a significant amount of hostility between the Pentecostal/Charismatic camp and the Evangelical/Fundamentalist camp. We weren't worried about unity as much as about superiority and being doctrinally right. Today, I believe God wants us to be more sensitive to things which could be stumbling blocks to the unity of the Spirit, which we are instructed to preserve (Ephesians 4:3).

Another designation or church name which has a ring of superiority is the common "First _____ Church." This applies equally to both camps. If the last shall be first and the first last, then maybe we should name our church the "Last _____ Church." Again, I am being a little picky, but I think it's good to think about how we are perceived by others when we use a name or term to describe ourselves. For what reason would we call ourselves the "First Church"? In some larger cities we find the "Second" and "Third" churches of various denominations. Perhaps I am missing the reason for thus naming a church, but it seems to me we are just finding our place in the "pecking order" when we do this.

PAUL TEACHES IMPORTANCE OF POWER

Another very significant teaching from Scripture dealing with the miraculous is found in the first four chapters of I Corinthians. After bringing up the problem situation of the divisions in the church, Paul pleads for unity and reminds them that he was not sent to make disciples after himself or baptize a lot of people. He declares:

"For Christ did not send me to baptize, but to preach the gospel, **not with wisdom of words, lest the cross of Christ should be made of no effect.** *For* **the message of the cross** *is foolishness to those who are perishing, but to us who are being saved it* **is the power of God."** *(I Corinthians 1:17,18)*

Notice the words I have highlighted in this well-known passage. Paul was sent to preach, but he clearly declared that his preaching was not about eloquence with words (even though he probably could have been extremely eloquent). Rather, he was saying that if he simply preached with words without God's power being demonstrated, that he would actually make the cross of Christ of no effect.

Another translation of "making the cross of no effect" is **"pouring out its power"**. Paul was saying that if he just preached with words he would be emptying or pouring out the power of the cross. Then Paul states that **the message of the cross . . . is the power of God.**

What an awesome truth! What the message of the cross is all about is God's power. What we should preach is that God used the cross to reveal the power of His love and that those who embrace that cross find His power and love released in them. When I die with Christ, I am also made a partaker of His resurrection, which is the epitome and supreme demonstration of His own awesome power.

The word for "power" is the Greek word "dunamis", from which we get the word "dynamite". This is often translated miracle and represents that supernatural power that is equated with signs and wonders.

Following the above-quoted two verses Paul adds:

"For it is written: 'I will destroy the wisdom of the wise, and bring to nothing the understanding of the prudent.'" *(I Corinthians 1:19)*

Our own wisdom if not empowered by the Holy Spirit will come to nothing. Only that which flows from Him will produce eternal results. Paul goes on to reveal the foolishness of worldly wisdom and then begins again to deal with the issue of signs and wisdom. Please read carefully the following few verses:

*"For since in the wisdom of God, the world through wisdom did not know God, it pleased God through the foolishness of the message preached to save **those who believe**." (I Corinthians 1:21)*

Notice that the message of the cross that Paul preached seemed foolish to the world's wisdom, but that those who would believe, in spite of its apparent foolishness would find it to be the power of God.

Now, please notice the following two verses, which relate directly to the subject of this book:

*"For **Jews request a sign**, and Greeks seek after wisdom; but we preach Christ crucified, to the Jews a stumbling block and to the Greeks, foolishness." (I Corinthians 1:22,23)*

Here again, we find Jews seeking for a sign, which God won't give them (because of wrong motives), while the Greeks are looking for something that makes sense to the mind or intellect. We are once again reminded that people respond differently. Greeks, in Jesus' day valued wisdom, while the Jews valued the supernatural. But notice now what Paul concludes:

"but to those who are called, both Jews and Greeks, Christ, the power of God and the wisdom of God." (I Corinthians 1:24)

To those who are called, there is no difference between the two. Both Jews and Greeks see Christ as the "Power of God" and the "Wisdom of God." Through the power of the Holy Spirit, Jesus is revealed as Power and as Wisdom.

REAFFIRMING OUR THESIS

Those who seek signs and wonders for the wrong motives will not receive them and those who seek wisdom for the wrong motives will find themselves being foolish, as is demonstrated in Romans 1, where it is recorded that people who thought themselves to be wise actually became as fools.

But to those who have hearts and minds open to the truth of God, He will reveal Himself in both power and wisdom. In fact, we have seen that He actually delights in us asking Him for signs and wonders as well as for fresh revelation, if we have a heart for His Kingdom and for an intimate relationship with Him.

WISDOM AND POWER – CONTINUED

The first chapter of I Corinthians ends with the well-known discussion of how God has chosen weak, simple and base things of this world to amaze the strong, wise and noble. He delights in turning our concepts inside-out and upside-down. His ways and thoughts are much higher than ours, so instead of choosing the most naturally gifted people, He often chooses those with less natural gifting and reveals His own power. As Paul says:

"That no flesh should glory in His presence." (I Corinthians 1:29)

It's very clear here, and throughout Scripture, that God does the supernatural in order to clearly reveal that He is God, so that man won't be as prone to take the glory.

MORE CONFIRMATION

Paul moves into the next chapter (chapter divisions, of course, were not in his original writings), without changing the subject. The first word is "And". Paul clearly declares that when he came to them, he didn't show off his oratorical skills, but rather he came with weakness, fear and much trembling. He also makes clear that he wants to focus on nothing but Jesus Christ and Him crucified. In verse four he amplifies his point with the following proclamation:

*"And my speech and my preaching were not with persuasive words of human wisdom, but in the **demonstration of the Spirit and of power, that your faith should not be in the wisdom of men, but in the power of God**."* (I Corinthians 2:4,5)

As we will see in Acts 18, there is no record of any particular miracle performed in Paul's visit to Corinth, but the above Scripture makes it clear that Paul was not just teaching or debating. He also must have revealed God's power with many demonstrations of the Spirit of God, as he clearly declares.

The conclusion or statement of purpose given by Paul was that his weakness of speech and focus on the power of the Spirit of God was specifically so that people would not put their faith in a person, but in the power of God. The Corinthian Greeks were philosophers like most of the Greeks and loved to hear and debate novel ideas. They, like we, could easily exalt and put their faith in a man who appears to be very wise. But Paul wanted their faith to be only in the power of God and not on his personal wisdom.

ONE MORE TIME

After this discussion of wisdom and power, Paul moves on to other subjects. But before the end of I Corinthians 4, Paul refers back to the same subject. Notice the intensity of his words:

"But I will come to you shortly, if the Lord wills, and I will know, not the word of those who are puffed up, but the power. For the kingdom of God is not in word but in power." (I Corinthians 4:19,20)

We know the importance of the spoken word, when it is anointed by God. But the point that Paul is making, is that **talk is cheap**, but those who really know God should be able to back it up with a demonstration of His power.

DIVINE DISCIPLINE PRODUCES DISCIPLE

Paul's first recorded convert on his first missionary journey with Barnabas was a man named Sergius Paulus, a proconsul, and "an intelligent man". He actually sought them out to hear the word of God. But a man known as Elymas, the sorcerer, who obviously didn't want Sergius Paulus to convert to Christianity, worked hard to disrupt them and turn away the seeker from truth.

But the Holy Spirit came powerfully upon Paul and he unleashed a holy verbal barrage that pronounced a sentence of temporary blindness on the surprised sorcerer. Elymas, seeing only that his sorcery had been overpowered totally by the superior power of God, immediately was reduced to a blind beggar, looking for someone to lead him by the hand.

The result was recorded by Luke:

"Then the proconsul believed, when he saw what had been done, being astonished at the teaching of the Lord." (I Corinthians 13:12)

Sergius Paulus was interested and hungry for the truth before the sentence of blindness on Elymas, but **the supernatural discipline was the convincing sign** to him that Paul and Barnabas were the authentic messengers of the truth of God.

ANTIOCH IN PISIDIA – NO RECORDED SIGNS

Paul and Barnabas proceeded to Antioch in Pisidia, where Paul preached in the synagogue to both Jew and Gentile. The Gentiles, along with many of the Jews, followed Paul and Barbabus and begged them to return the next Sabbath.

While there is no record of any miraculous occurrence in this city, there is evidence that the people were excited about something. Notice Luke's remarks:

"And the next Sabbath almost the whole city came together to hear the word of God." (Acts 13:44)

Perhaps the good news of the gospel was so exciting to them that they came en masse because of that and that alone. But according to Paul's own testimony, he had fully preached the gospel with signs and wonders accompanying his words, from Jerusalem to the farthest reaches of his ministry, in order to make the Gentiles obedient to the faith. (Romans 15:18,19)

Thus we have no hard evidence that signs and wonders had any impact on the multitudes of people who came and accepted Jesus as Savior in Antioch in Pisidia. But because of Paul's statement in Romans 15, we wouldn't want to ignore the strong possibility that signs and wonders were actually performed by the Holy Spirit through Paul and Barnabas, but were not considered unusual or significant enough to be recorded by Luke.

SIGNS AND WONDERS PRODUCE RESULTS IN ICONIUM CRUSADE

Luke's record of the apostles' next crusade leaves no doubt about the involvement of signs and wonders in bringing people to faith. Please read the following passage:

> *"Now it happened in Iconium that they went together to the synagogue of the Jews, **and so spoke that a great multitude both of the Jews and of the Greeks believed.** But the unbelieving Jews stirred up the Gentiles and poisoned their minds against the brethren. Therefore they stayed there a long time, **speaking boldly in the Lord, who was bearing witness to the word of His grace, granting signs and wonders to be done by their hands."** (Acts 14:1-3)*

In the first verse we read that they "so spoke" that many believed. The third verse says they were "speaking boldly in the Lord, who was bearing witness to the word of His grace, granting signs and wonders to be done by their hands."

It may be only speculation, but does the expression, "so spoke" refer to clever oratory or shouting and pulpit pounding? Or could it rather refer to the fact that they were speaking boldly as a result of the signs and wonders which were being done? Remember, when the apostles prayed for boldness in Acts 4. They asked for signs and wonders to be done to give them boldness. (Acts 4:29,30)

According to I Corinthians 2:1-5, Paul did not come with fancy words or powerful speech when he ministered to the Corinthians. Perhaps his approach was different in Iconium, but chances are, his philosophy was similar in all the cities where he ministered.

MIRACLE IN LYSTRA GETS SURPRISE RESPONSE

When the hostile Jews stirred up the crowds to stone the apostles, they quickly fled to Lystra, where they preached the gospel. Luke gives the following account:

"And in Lystra a certain man without strength in his feet was sitting, a cripple from his mother's womb, who had never walked. This man heard Paul speaking. Paul observing him intently, and seeing that he had faith to be healed, said with a loud voice, 'Stand on your feet!' And he leaped and walked."

Again, we are not given any details about Paul's message, but it is noteworthy that the crippled man had faith to believe for a miracle. My personal deduction is that Paul must have preached about the healing power of Jesus. He may have even given his own personal testimony of his encounter with Jesus, which included being blind and then healed again.

Normally, people receive or have faith for salvation after they have heard about the salvation power of Jesus. Of course, that faith is greatly encouraged when they see some evidence that God is real. Even so people will have more faith for healing or other needs when they hear about the miracle power of Jesus. The more we are exposed to truth, the more it becomes reality to us.

Personally, I was raised to believe in the miraculous power of God. I was exposed to the message of the supernatural power of Jesus through my Bible reading, biographies, revival meetings, powerful testimonies of others and the occasional gospel movie. My parents had an unusual walk of faith, and I have found it much easier to trust God in times of testing than most Christians who have not had this kind of training in a life of faith.

But let's move on to the surprise consequences of the healing of the lame man:

"Now when the people saw what Paul had done, they raised their voices, saying in the Lycaonian language, 'The gods have

*come down to us in the likeness of men!' And Barnabas they called
Zeus, and Paul, Hermes, because he was the chief speaker. Then
the priest of Zeus, whose temple was in front of their city, brought
oxen and garlands to the gates, intending to sacrifice with the
multitudes."*

I guess we could say, as far as creating faith is concerned, the healing
of the cripple was a major act of overkill. The natives of Lystra obviously
had not heard or digested enough of the teaching about Jesus to properly interpret the message of the sign, given by God through Paul.

We must remember to keep a focus on the message and use the
sign to reinforce or validate the message. **We are not called to focus
on the sign, but rather to read the message of the sign and respond
to it. But the preaching and teaching of the gospel must always
be the focus. The point we are making here is that when we
have the right motives, the sign will add power to the preaching
and teaching.** It will not detract from it or take the attention away
from the spoken word.

Of course, Paul quickly tried to correct their faulty interpretation
of the sign miracle, and stopped the people from sacrificing to them.
But the jealous Jews, from whom Paul and Barnabas had escaped in
the previous city, quickly caught up with them and persuaded the
multitude to stone Paul. They brutally stoned him and dragged him
out of the city, supposing him to be dead. We are not told if he was
actually dead or not, but when the disciples gathered around him,
he rose up and went into the city.

DERBE HEARS THE GOSPEL

The day after Paul's stoning, he departed from Lystra, apparently
completely well, and headed for Derbe. There Paul and Barnabas
preached the gospel and "made many disciples". Again, there are no
details given. We have only Paul's previously mentioned testimony
that he fully preached the gospel from Jerusalem to Illyricum by
performing signs and wonders in the name of Jesus.

After the ministry in Derbe, the apostolic duo revisited the cities where they had just previously been and strengthened the disciples. They also appointed elders in every church and prayed and fasted with them before returning to Antioch, their home base.

PAUL BEGINS SECOND JOURNEY

After participating in a big leadership meeting in Jerusalem, Paul took Silas as his new partner, while Barnabas took Mark and journeyed to Cyprus. Paul retraced his steps through Syria and Cilicia, "strengthening the churches." (Acts 15:41).

During this time they shared the decisions made by the council in Jerusalem. Luke describes the results of their ministry:

"So the churches were strengthened in the faith, and increased in number daily." (Acts 16:5)

Here we have another case of no direct evidence of the supernatural, yet the churches continue to grow, which obviously means that people are becoming believers. Again, we can speculate that there were probably miraculous happenings, based on Paul's testimony in Romans, but we have no specific proof for this case.

MACEDONIAN CALL FOR PAUL

Paul and Silas's mission to Macedonia was in contrast with the previous record filled with a variety of supernatural events. First of all the Holy Spirit in some way made it clear to Paul that he was not to journey to two different regions that he had thought would be a good idea. In Troas, Paul saw a vision of a Macedonian man calling for help. Paul realized that God was redirecting his steps, through a supernatural occurrence, and headed for Philippi.

In Philippi, at the river side, they met for prayer and spoke to the women there. A seller of purple, named Lydia, listened to the gospel. She was already a worshipper of God, and Luke reports that:

"The Lord opened her heart to heed the things spoken by Paul." (Acts 16:14)

Here was a lady, who didn't need any sign or wonder to convince her. She was a worshipper and knew by the Spirit that these were men of God. Their message rang true as God opened her obedient heart to receive from Paul.

But unclean spiritual powers began to oppose Paul through a fortune-telling slave girl, who had made her masters a small fortune through this "spirit of divination". She followed Paul around, pretending to be on his side, probably hoping to become a leader of his new following. She boldly proclaimed Paul and company to be "servants of the Most High God".

Finally, after many days, Paul had enough and he commanded the unclean spirit to come out of her. She immediately lost her power of divination and her masters were very angry at Paul and Silas, and had them thrown in jail.

JOYFUL JAILBIRDS

The next miraculous event was the joy displayed in jail by Paul and Silas as they sang and worshipped at midnight, while the other prisoners listened. But what really convinced the jailer was an 8.0 earthquake that opened the jails and loosed the chains of all the prisoners.

The jailer, assuming his prisoners had fled, and that he would lose his head as a result, drew his sword to take his own life before someone else could. Paul and Silas, again showing the difference between a Christian's attitude and that of an unbeliever, had not fled. Instead they called out to the jailer to stop his potentially fatal response to the earthquake, assuring him that all his prisoners were still there.

The fact that the other prisoners didn't leave seems to imply that they too were becoming believers in the God who could give prisoners a song in the night and release them with a major earthquake in response to their worship. At any rate they did not flee the prison.

Luke reports the jailer's response and Paul's reply:

"Then he called for a light, ran in, and fell down trembling before Paul and Silas. And he brought them out and said, 'Sirs,

what must I do to be saved?' So they said, 'Believe on the Lord Jesus Christ, and you will be saved, you and your household.'" (Acts 16:29-31)

You know God is moving in your midst when people approach you to ask you how to get saved. The jailer and his whole household believed in Jesus and were baptized that very day. The obvious reason for their salvation was the miraculous chain of events which occurred that night. Of course, the character of the joyful jail-birds was a contributing factor, but the earthquake was certainly the clincher that closed the deal for the Holy Spirit.

GREEKS SEEK AFTER WISDOM

Paul ministered in four cities on the Greek peninsula. They were Thessolonica, Berea, Athens and Corinth. The most interesting thing for our study is the fact that there were no reported public miracles in Luke's account of Paul's ministry in these four cities. But two of these cities, Thessolonica and Corinth, were later sent epistles that referred to the supernatural happenings there. We cannot prove that he would have said similar things to the Bereans and Athenians, had he written them epistles as well, but there is a good probability that he would have, based on his testimony in Romans.

As we have already pointed out, Paul declared that when he was in Corinth, he didn't come with the wisdom of man, but "in demonstration of the Spirit and power". (I Corinthians 2:4) This certainly implies signs and wonders.

In addition, if we read his first letter to the Thessalonians, we discover that his preaching there apparently was also with signs and wonders. Note his comments to them:

*"For our gospel did not come to you in word only, **but also in power, and in the Holy Spirit** and in much assurance, as you know what kind of men we were among you for your sake." (I Thessalonians 1:5)*

Obviously, the absence of specific mention in Luke's record does not prove that no signs and wonders occurred, but it does appear that the Greeks, who "seek after wisdom" (I Corinthians 1:22) were perhaps more impressed by logic than by the miraculous. Thus Luke focused on Paul's primary method of reaching the Greek mind.

1. Faith and Paranoia

The first city encountered on the Greek Peninsula was Thessolonica, where Paul and his team went to the Jewish synagogue and,

"reasoned from the Scriptures, explaining and demonstrating that the Christ had to suffer and rise again from the dead, and saying, 'This Jesus whom I preach to you is the Christ.' And some of them were persuaded; and a great multitude of the devout Greeks, and not a few of the leading women, joined Paul and Silas." (Acts 17:2-4)

Here again we find "some" of the people, and "a great multitude of the devout Greeks" believed as a result of Paul's opening the Scripture to them. We know that Paul's letter to them declares that his preaching was not with word only but with power, and the Holy Spirit. Again, when we put this reference with Paul's testimony in Romans 15:19, we have significant evidence that miracles took place to help bring people to faith.

Now when enough of the local unbelieving Jews began to make things hot for the apostles, they slipped away to their next assignment.

2. Bereans Receive Paul with Open Hearts and Minds

Arriving in Berea, the apostles again visited the local synagogue and taught the people. Luke gives us his appraisal of the Bereans:

"These were more fair-minded than those in Thessolonica, in that they received the word with all readiness, and searched the Scriptures daily to find out whether these things were so. Therefore many of them believed, and also not a few of the Greeks, prominent women as well as men." (Acts 17:11,12)

These positive results in Berea reveal that those with open minds and hearts will accept the gospel when presented by an anointed servant of God, who has an anointing to understand and teach the Word of God. Again there is no direct evidence of the supernatural contributing to the Bereans' faith, but we know that it would be the exception if no signs and wonders occurred. In addition, Paul often shared his own supernatural conversion, the supernatural ministry of Jesus, and no doubt shared about other miracles he had seen as well.

At any rate, it wasn't long until the hostile unbelieving Jews from Thessalonica heard the news that Paul and Silas were in Berea. They hurried over to Berea and quickly stirred up the opposition again. As a result, Paul was shipped off to Athens, while Silas and Timothy stayed back with the new converts and headed for Athens later.

3. Athenians Check Out the Latest Philosophy

Paul attended the synagogue in Athens and began to reason with both the Jewish and Gentile worshippers. He also shared his faith in the marketplace and aroused the interest of the philosophers in the city, who wanted to hear more from this "babbler", who was preaching about what they called, "foreign gods".

After a crowd gathered, Paul talked to them about an altar he had seen dedicated to "The Unknown God", and preached about Jesus. Luke tells us:

"And when they heard of the resurrection of the dead, some mocked, while others said, 'We will hear you again on this matter.' So Paul departed from among them. However, some men joined him and believed, among them Dionysius the Areopagite, a woman named Damaris, and others with them." (Acts 17:32-34)

Once again, we have no clear record of any miracle, and we have apparently not too many converts among the supposedly wise philosophers of Athens. But some were convinced and made Paul's time in Athens worth while.

4. Corinth Given the Gospel

Paul journeyed to Corinth ahead of Silas and Timothy and began to reason in the Synagogue every Sabbath, and "persuaded both Jews and Greeks." (Acts 18:4)   But Paul was especially burdened "by the Spirit" for the Jews in Corinth and proclaimed that Jesus was the Christ. When they vehemently rejected the gospel, Paul declared that their blood was on their own heads and that he would focus on the Gentiles.

Then Paul went to stay with a brother named Justus, who lived next door to the synagogue. Through this arrangement Paul was able to bring to faith a Gentile named Crispus, who was the "ruler of the synagogue". His whole household was converted and Luke also records:

"And many of the Corinthians, hearing, believed and were baptized." (Acts 18:8)

Following this we are told that the Lord spoke to Paul in a vision, revealing to him that he would not be attacked in Corinth and that he should be bold and keep preaching the gospel. As a result of this personal sign to Paul, he stayed a year and six months before departing.

As we stated above, there were no public signs and wonders recorded by Luke in the four cities on the Greek Peninsula. This vision, which was a sign to Paul was the one near-exception. But from Paul's own testimony, which we discussed above, we know that Paul did demonstrate the power of God.

EPHESUS ABOUNDS IN SIGNS AND WONDERS

Holy Spirit Empowers New Converts

When Paul arrived in Ephesus, he found disciples of John the Baptist, who hadn't heard the gospel of Jesus Christ. After leading them to faith in Jesus and baptizing them they experienced the power of the Holy Spirit, as recorded by Luke:

"And when Paul had laid hands on them, the Holy Spirit came upon them, and they spoke with tongues and prophesied." (Acts 19:6)

Thus the converts were quickly introduced to the supernatural power of the Holy Spirit. This experience would naturally encourage their faith and get them excited about proclaiming the gospel to others. Paul again began ministering in the synagogues until the Jews rejected the gospel. He continued to teach on a daily basis in "the school of Tyrannus" for a period of two years.

Special Miracles Performed

It was in Ephesus where probably the most interesting miracle activity in Paul's ministry took place. Luke describes it this way:

*"Now God worked unusual miracles by the hand of Paul, **so that even** handkerchiefs or aprons were brought from his body to the sick, and the **diseases left them and the evil spirits went out of them.**" (Acts 19:11,12)*

The phrase "so that even" indicates that many other unusual miracles occurred, but these mentioned were probably the most unusual. Note that people were both healed and delivered from demonic power, through the anointing that was transferred to the sick via the pieces of cloth which were first touched by Paul.

Luke doesn't tell us immediately about the effect of these miracles as far as bringing others to faith is concerned, but rather waits until he has related the next story.

Itinerant Exorcists Make Hasty Exit

A number of "itinerant Jewish exorcists" including seven sons of a Jewish chief priest, named Sceva, tried to use the name of Jesus, "whom Paul preaches" to deliver a man under the influence of evil spirits. Read Luke's narrative of the results of their attempt to imitate Paul's ministry without his anointing:

*"And the evil spirit answered and said, 'Jesus I know, and Paul I know; but who are you?' Then the man in whom the evil spirit was leaped on them, overpowered them, and prevailed against them, so that they fled out of that house naked and wounded. **This became known both to all Jews and Greeks dwelling in Ephesus; and fear fell on them all, and the name of the Lord Jesus was magnified."** (Acts 19:15-17)*

This story graphically illustrates what happens when God's power is pitted against the power of Satan or compared with the powerlessness of religion without the anointing. Paul's ministry had produced some powerful miracles that let everyone know that Jesus was still alive and operating through His body on the earth. And when people were delivered from demonic power, it showed that the servants of Jesus had more power than the servants of Satan.

But when the most religious Jews tried to do the same thing, they revealed their own lack of power over the power of the enemy. The result was that Jesus was magnified in the eyes of all the people and the fear of the Lord was on them all. In addition Luke makes it very clear that the fame of this incident spread to the whole city. No amount of advertising could have spread the word as efficiently as one such unusual demonstration of supernatural power.

Big Bonfire Burns Bad Books

Luke continues to describe the results of these exciting events in Ephesus:

*"And many who had believed came confessing and telling their deeds. Also, many of those who had practiced magic brought their books together and burned them in the sight of all. And they counted up the value of them, and it totaled fifty thousand pieces of silver. ($364,000) **So the word of the Lord grew mightily and prevailed.** (Acts 19:19,20)*

The value of the satanic materials burned is a good indication of how many people were converted through the ministry of Paul and his team. What is even more significant is the fact that the contest of power between God and Satan produced a multitude of conversions among those who had been serving Satan.

As I mentioned earlier, when the Harry Potter occultic phenomenon hit the movie theaters, I began advocating the production of a major movie depicting the book of Acts, featuring the frequent demonstrations of the superior power of God over the power of sorcerers, etc. We who know Him whose power is so much greater than Satan's should not let a movie like Harry Potter go unchallenged.

WRAPPING UP PAUL'S MINISTRY

There were several more miracles or references to the supernatural in the last few chapters of Acts, including the raising of a young man from the dead, but these cases deal mainly with people who are already believers and there are no recorded conversions as a result.

It is important to point out here that signs, wonders and miracles were done for two main reasons. **The first reason is to reveal the power of God, with the result that people will believe in Him.** This of course is the subject of this book. But it is not the only purpose for the miraculous.

The second reason for the miraculous is that God cares about the people He created. He has compassion on those who suffer. This is recorded in many places in Scripture. God sent Moses to His people in Egypt because He had heard their groaning and was coming to deliver them. Jesus repeatedly had compassion on the multitude and ministered to them, even when He was tired and wanted to rest.

This point is important, because even if God had changed His mind about doing miracles to help people believe, He would also have had to change His character to not have compassion of those who suffer, in order for Him to decree that miracles are no longer for today. Now let's get back to the biblical record.

Snake Attack Opens Door to Ministry

After Paul's arrest in Jerusalem, he was transported to Rome by ship. Before their departure, he had clearly prophesied dangerous weather, but the Roman centurion listened to the helmsman and the owner of the ship more than to Paul. When Paul's prophecy came true, the attitudes changed toward Paul and his next warnings were heeded.

After the ship was ruined, but their lives were spared, as prophesied by the word of the Lord through Paul, they landed on an island called Malta. Here we find another explosion of miracles that produced faith in those who observed.

First Paul was bitten by a viper which came out of the bonfire that had been built to dry off the victims of the shipwreck. The natives, knowing he was a prisoner, assumed that he was being punished for his crimes. When he suffered no harm, they changed their minds and thought that he was a god.

We are not given any information about what freedom Paul had to preach to them, but the next event was the healing of the father of Publius, the most prominent citizen of the island. Luke reports the following:

"And it happened that the father of Publius lay sick of a fever and dysentery. Paul went in to him and prayed, and he laid his hands on him and healed him. So when this was done, the rest of those on the island who had diseases also came and were healed."
(Acts 28:8,9)

While there is no plain declaration that the natives were converted to faith in Jesus, experience would tell us that it would be very unusual for them not to have accepted Jesus as Savior, as well as healer. It seems that Paul must have been given freedom to preach, if he was given the freedom to lay hands on all the sick folks. This would have been Paul's last great harvest before his incarceration in Rome.

Some Believe Paul in Prison

Paul was given a private place in prison, while under the supervision of a prison guard. Before long a group of Jews living in Rome came to visit him to find out what Christianity was all about. Paul clearly shared the message of the gospel to them, preaching Jesus from the Law and the Prophets, with the following results:

"And some were persuaded by the things which were spoken, and some disbelieved." (Acts 28:24)

Some did believe, apparently through the anointing on Paul's spoken words, but some did not. But when they couldn't agree, Paul rebuked the unbelief of the Jewish people and told them that God had granted salvation to the Gentiles and that the Gentiles would believe.

Paul remained for two years in Rome, freely preaching and teaching those who came to him. We have no record of any further miracles or conversions in his ministry, but what we have already learned has been very helpful in our pursuit of an understanding of the relationship between the miraculous and transforming faith.

CHAPTER 11

End-Time Power of Signs

SIGNS OF THE BEAST HAVE POWER TO DECEIVE

Another Scripture regarding signs and belief comes in the book of Revelation. Chapter thirteen tells us about the antichrist, or the "beast". John describes the coming of a second, "beast".

"Then I saw another beast coming up out of the earth, and he had two horns like a lamb and spoke like a dragon. And he exercises all the authority of the first beast in his presence, and causes the earth and those who dwell in it to worship the first beast, whose deadly wound was healed.

"He performs great signs, so that he even makes fire come down from heaven on the earth in the sight of men. And he deceives those who dwell on the earth by those signs which he was granted to do in the sight of the beast, ..." *(Revelation 13:11-14)*

A similar passage is found in Matthew 24:24, where Jesus said,

"For false christs and false prophets will arise and show great signs and wonders, so as to deceive, if possible, even the elect." *(Matthew 24:24)*

The power to deceive is clearly the power to convince or produce a kind of faith in someone, even though it may be a misguided faith.

In the Revelation passage **the beast will cause people on the earth to believe in him because of the signs he produces.**

Clearly, signs and wonders do not unequivocally prove that a person is from God. We know that the Egyptian magicians could perform signs and wonders themselves, in response to the signs done by Moses. There are two sources of miracle power, and they are competing with each other to produce the maximum number of converts to their side.

The point of this whole study is to show that signs and wonders do produce belief, and that God has given us superior power to perform signs and wonders to produce as much faith in God as possible. If we allow the New Age and occultic religions and psychics to reveal their limited power without showing them up like Moses and Paul did, then we are allowing our enemy to take advantage of us and produce more converts than we do.

Instead, based on the overwhelming evidence that we have examined, we should earnestly seek God for the complete restoration of His power to the church of the twenty-first century, in order that we be fully equipped to bring in His great end-time harvest. Today's harvest field is so very ripe and waiting for the harvesters who have learned to use the powerful harvesting tools that the Lord of the harvest has provided for them.

We have too long tried to combat the powers of darkness with theology or rational arguments. God has always combated the powers of darkness with the power of light. Supernatural signs were countered with more powerful supernatural signs. Again remember Moses and Aaron and Peter and Paul in their various encounters with sorcerers, etc. Power was conquered by a greater power. Hate is conquered by love. Satanic power to curse is conquered by God's power to bless. As was shared with me by a scholarly friend, Maurice Fuller, a retired Canadian pastor and Bible School professor, doctrinal attacks are refuted with Scripture, but attacks in the realm of the supernatural, should be combated with superior supernatural power.

CHAPTER 12

Assimilating Our Biblical Data

DIVIDING INTO CATEGORIES

My clear intention at this point was to assign each biblical instance of belief to one of three categories. With a strong desire to be fair and honest I made a concerted effort to do so.

But I quickly discovered that because of the many different types of miraculous occurrences and because of the uncertainty of several of the passages, it was becoming very difficult to put many of the faith occurrences into one category or the other. There were some occasions, where it was obvious that people became believers, but it wasn't clear if that happened before or after they had seen a miracle.

Also, it would be reasonable to think that almost everyone who already had faith when they came to Jesus for a healing or other miracle had by that time heard from others about the miracles Jesus had performed. The same would hold true for the apostles. Even when no miracles are mentioned, the most likely scenario is that miracles were talked about during the process of communicating the gospel.

Every recorded message in the book of Acts refers to something supernatural, including fulfilled prophecy, the miracles of Jesus, Paul's miraculous conversion and other supernatural events. Even Paul's message on Mars Hill in Athens ends up talking about the resurrection of Jesus.

There were cases in both the Old and New Testament, where we can be quite certain that people from outside the family of God heard about the power of God and became believers, but we have no conclusive documented proof. Some, like Publius and the others on the Island of Malta, doubtless became believers after seeing the various miracles take place, but Luke does not give us that information.

People came to Egypt for grain and certainly must have heard the story of Joseph's dream interpretation and divine wisdom, but we have no record that anyone believed. We know that people came to hear the supernatural wisdom of Solomon, and must have heard him credit his God, but we have no record of Gentile conversions. We know that the Queen of Sheba was overwhelmed with what she witnessed first hand, but we have no record that she worshipped Jehovah, and left her other gods, even though she extolled the God of Solomon.

GENERAL CONCLUSIONS

With the above explanation, let me give my personal interpretation of the extensive data that we have covered in this biblical research.

I. Virtually no person or group of persons came to faith without at least hearing about the supernatural power of God.

II. Of the nearly 100 cases we have looked at since the days of Noah, 90-95% or more appear to have believed after having personally witnessed an element of the supernatural.

III. At least 10 times, kings and other rulers of cities, nations or empires believed in God because of a demonstration of divine power.

IV. At least 5 times, whole nations were convinced that Jehovah was the true and living God because of a miraculous event.

V. At least 22 more times, other groups of people, including "great multitudes" turned to God at the same time because He had demonstrated His power to them.

We will add some other observations and try to strike a realistic balance when we come to our final conclusion. But we trust that these first five statements will give the reader a clear picture of what was normal for God's people in biblical times, as far as bringing unbelievers to faith was concerned.

At this point, we would like to move on to the task of applying this biblical model to modern day Christianity, especially in western culture, with its scientific, anti-supernatural mind-set.

CHAPTER 13

A Glimpse of Relevant Church History

There were many great leaders of the church who carried on the work of spreading the gospel and bringing people to faith in Jesus after the original apostles passed away. The information available to us does not give us an overabundance of material directly relevant to this study. However there have been many writers who gave us little nuggets of information that provide clear evidence to support the thesis of this book.

The bulk of the relevant information that we have gathered simply makes the emphatic statement that miraculous events continued to occur in the various forms of Christianity that developed in the centuries following biblical times. There was certainly a decline in frequency and later a perversion of the whole meaning and purpose of the miraculous, but there was never a time period of any length in which the miraculous was not recorded.

The problem for our study is that most of the records do not report the results of the signs and wonders with respect to the number of people who were brought to faith in Christ. But we do have the fact that there was parallel and continuous growth in the church, even during great persecution. People were being brought to faith continuously, at the same time as the reports of signs and wonders were going on. This would be a case of coincidence and speculation if we did not have the overwhelming evidence of Scripture, which we have already examined.

People have always responded to the miraculous. They did in Moses' time, in Jesus time, in the days of the first Apostles, and they still do today as we shall see in the next chapter. There is no reason to believe that they did not respond to the miraculous with faith in God during the centuries which followed the foundation of the early church.

Irenaeus lived in the latter half of the second century and reported events that confirm that the miraculous was still happening. In addition, he makes a comment which directly confirms our thesis. He wrote:

> " . . . true disciples having received grace from him use it in his name for the benefit of the rest of men, even as each has received the gift from him. For some drive out demons with certainty and truth, so that often <u>those who have themselves been cleansed from the evil spirits believe and are in the church</u>, and some have fore-knowledge of things to be, and visions and prophetic speech, and others cure the sick by the laying on of hands and make them whole, and even as we have said, the dead have been raised and remained with us for many years. And why should I say more? It is not possible to tell the number of the gifts which the church throughout the whole world, having received them from God in the name of Jesus Christ, who was crucified under Pontius Pilate, uses each day for the benefit of the heathen, deceiving none and making profit from none. For as it received freely from God, it ministers also freely."[1]

This is one of the rare clear statements that miraculous events produce belief and faithful Christians, who remain in the church. It also reveals that all kinds of miraculous signs and wonders were taking place in the second century.

Another quote which clearly supports our thesis is by Philip Schaff.

"Tertullian attributes many if not most of the conversions of his day to supernatural dreams and visions, as does also Origen, although with more caution."[2] We could at this point overwhelm the reader with quotes from numerous excellent historical works, which we have researched and made notes from and which would powerfully confirm the fact that signs and wonders continued to take place in the early centuries of Christianity. However, we don't want to discourage the average reader from finishing this book, so we will give a brief summary of our research.

The following literary sources and church leaders made significant and clear statements to confirm the continuity of the miraculous following the biblical record:

1. The Syrian writings of the first century known as the *Didache*.
2. Clement of Rome (end of first century)
3. Ignatius of Antioch (between A. D. 98 and 117)
4. Justin Martyr (died a martyr between A. D. 162 and 168)
5. Origen (greatest of the Greek writers)
6. Irenaeus (latter half of the second century)
7. Eusebius of Caesarea (died around A. D. 340)
8. Novatian – a prominent elder (came close to becoming Bishop of Rome in A.D. 251)
9. Tertullian of Carthage – a church writer who wrote from A.D. 197 to 217
10. Cyprian – a bishop of Carthage (became a Christian about A.D. 245, beheaded for faith in A.D. 258)
11. Augustine (354-430) (one of the greatest Christian theologians of all time)

The actual statements made by these early church leaders can be read in the following books:

1. *Charismatic Gifts in the Early Church* by Ronald A. N. Kydd (Peabody, Massachusettes, Hendrickson Publishers Inc., 1984)

2. *Divine Healing Through the Centuries* by J. Sidlow Baxter (Grand Rapids Michigan, Zondervan Publishing House, 1979)

3. *History of the Christian Church – Volume II* by Philip Schaff (Grand Rapids Michigan, Wm. B. Eerdmans Publishing Company, 1910)

4. *Signs of Revival* by Dr. Patrick Dixon (Kingsway Publications Ltd, Eastbourne, Great Britain, 1994)

J. Sidlow Baxter, in summing up the information he discovered in his research, made the following statement on pages 100, 101 of the book referenced above:

"I shall not hesitate to say that in my own opinion there is ample evidence through sufficiently trustworthy witnesses to establish the fact that direct divine healing of the body has been taught, experienced, observed, and faithfully reported among Christian believers, at intervals longer or shorter, right from post-Apostolic times until now. However cleverly some of the testimony may be devaluated (supposedly), more than enough remains which is unimpeachable."[3]

Dr. Patrick Dixon on page 118 of the above work, *Signs of Revival* made the following remarks:

"Even in the Dark Ages God gave some gracious revivals. From the twelfth to the fifteenth century there were revivals in Southern Europe in which many spoke in other tongues. Foremost among these revivalists were the Waldenses (12th *century in southern France and northern Italy) and Albigenses. The Encyclopedia Britannica states that the glossolalia (or speaking in tongues) 'recurs in Christian revivals of every age, e.g., among the friars of the thirteenth century, among the Jansenists and early Quakers, the persecuted Protestants of the Cevennes, and the Irvingites'."*

Dixon reports signs such as falling (often under conviction), laughing, crying, shaking, prophesying and speaking in tongues among numerous Christian leaders and movements since the beginning of the reformation. These included Francis Xavier, the Quakers, 'the inspired ones of the Wetterau' in Germany, John Wesley (who himself was overcome with laughter), Jonathan Edwards, George Whitefield, David Brainard, Charles Finney, the Salvation Army and numerous revivals in Great Britain.

Again we believe that the multitudes of conversions, which took place during the explosion of revivals under the above leaders and movements, were at least in part accelerated by the occurrence of the miraculous in their midst. We can make this assumption based on some anecdotal evidence, as well as on the fact that God's ways have not changed a lot over the centuries from Moses' time until the present, as we shall see in the next chapter.

CHAPTER 14

The Role of Signs and Wonders Today

A SAMPLING OF EVENTS FROM RECENT CHURCH HISTORY

AFRICA HARVEST IN FULL SWING

The most recent bit of information that I have come across relating to the subject of this book came on a Christian television broadcast. The host was interviewing Reinhart Bonnke, a German evangelist, who was educated in Britain and was commissioned by God to take the gospel to Africa. Bonnke's ongoing war-cry has been, "Africa shall be saved!"

In his younger days, Bonnke saw a vision of a blood-washed Africa. His crusades grew larger and larger until today they have become enormous. His meetings are highlighted by dramatic healings and miracles of all kinds.

A recent well-publicized miracle was the raising of a pastor from the dead. The man had been three days in the morgue after being certified dead by a medical doctor. The wife, knowing that Reinhart Bonnke was in town to dedicate a large church building, took him to the church in his coffin. She took his body out of the car and had it laid out on a table in the basement, under the sanctuary, where the meeting was going on.

Suddenly the pastor began to breathe and in a short time he was functioning normally. He began to tell of his visits to Heaven and

Hell. Much of his recovery was filmed on video by an amateur photographer. A documentary video has been released from the ministry, which features the witness of the doctor and family, etc.

The impact of miracles such as the above has been incredible. Bonnke reports that in the last three crusades about six million individuals have filled in cards indicating conversion to Christianity. He thus is anticipating about ten million conversions by the time he has finished the five scheduled major crusades for this crusade season.

A recent crusade in Lagos, Nigeria, drew crowds estimated between three and four million. Decision cards filled out in one meeting totaled over one million. The miracles that consistently occur in Bonnke's meetings have drawn the unsaved as nothing else has done in the history of mankind. Working his way from the south to the north, Reinhart Bonnke's miraculous and evangelistic ministry has powerfully impacted the continent of Africa.

Just as we have found in the pages of the Bible, when people see visible signs and wonders, they believe the message of the one who is being used by God to perform them. Especially where the gospel has not yet saturated the area, the excitement caused by the miraculous spreads like wildfire, and when people hear about it they come from far and near.

Bonnke is not the only one having great success in Africa. Reports are also coming from many others, who are also seeing great miracles, including the frequent raising of the dead. As a result their ministries are also growing rapidly in various parts of Africa.

Some reports maintain that if present trends continue, Sub-Saharan Africa could soon become the next center or hub of Christianity. These reports claim that soon over 50% of Africa will be Christian.

IRIS MINISTRIES

Rolland and Heidi Baker are witnessing one of the greatest evangelistic and church growth explosions in history, with a base of operations in the African nation of Mozambique. After many trials and tribulations in their missionary endeavors in different nations, God led them to this politically, economically and socially devastated nation on the southeast coast of Africa. They took over a very neglected and impoverished orphanage in Maputo, the capital city, and loved the children with sacrificial love. Then they started taking in children from the streets and the garbage dump in Maputo.They had been encountering God in some unusual ways in those days and believed God for supernatural miracles. These began to happen! Not only did they see miraculous healings, but other kinds of miracles, like the feeding of the two hundred children with four small bowls of food, took place on a regular basis.

Heidi had many intimate encounters with God, being taken to Heaven on several occasions. She there experienced the intimate love of Jesus and committed herself to bringing His love to everyone she could. Her faith led her to pray for many severe cases, including totally blind individuals. Miracles began to occur more and more.

After laboring like many missionaries to get a few converts and start a few churches, things began to explode in their region. Soon they were training pastors as quickly as possible to meet the demands for new churches. In less than five years, over six thousand new churches sprang up.

This is their normal method of starting new churches. Taking with them one of their young Bible School students, they fly or drive into a remote village. The crowd gathers either to see why the plane is there or because they hear the music and see the foreigners setting up their sound and video equipment.

Then the Jesus Film is shown and they begin to preach and pray for the sick. Invariably several miracles take place and the invitation to accept Christ is given. Many people accept Jesus as Savior and Lord and of course, they need a church and a pastor. The Bible College grad stays there and becomes their pastor. They have just planted another church.

Do the churches last? How well are they supervised and established, etc.? It seems that they are doing very well and continuing to grow.

At any rate, the Bakers don't claim to know how to handle the sudden growth. They just cry out to God for Him to give them wisdom and strength to keep up with the awesome growth. Their constant cry to God is, "Help us not to wreck it! Help us not to wreck it!"

In addition, they have expanded in many directions into other nations. They have personally seen thousands of Muslims, those considered the most difficult to convert, turning to Jesus by the thousands. They have discovered that showing Jesus love, whether they are ministering to one or ten thousand or more, Jesus does the miracles that win the hearts to Him. Readers are encouraged to read their testimony in a book called, "There is Always Enough".

Since writing this, I have made two trips to Mozambique and personally witnessed conferences, Bible Schools for pastors, a brand new on-site Missions School and several outreaches into unreached villages. In Northern Mozambique, in the city of Pemba, Arco Iris Ministries has a new base among what was the largest unreached tribe in all of Africa. Former Muslims are now converted by the thousands and the numbers are exploding with each new outreach. I personally witnessed around one thousand conversions and many miracles including about a dozen deaf mutes healed and several blind people healed, both young and old. Many other infirmities such as hernias and back problems were also healed, most of them instantly.

FRESH FIRE MINISTRIES

Another dynamic young minister of miracles is Todd Bentley. He is also spending much time in Africa and other nations of the world. His crusades have not yet rivaled that of Reinhart Bonkke, but at this writing, he is not yet thirty years old. Already huge crowds are gathering wherever he goes in Africa, and incredible miracles are happening. The result is always a multitude of souls brought into the kingdom.

Todd's youthful boldness is incredible. He has challenged Muslims to bring their toughest cases and if the first three don't get healed, he will go home and give up his faith in God. God has come through for him every time, because he first listens to God and speaks what he hears.

Todd Bentley didn't come into his ministry in the normal way. His salvation out of his drug and prison background was an unusually miraculous event. It wasn't long until he was spending eight or more hours a day seeking God and visiting Heaven. Today he teaches with incredible detail on Heavenly visitations and other Biblical experiences with God. The miracles are on the increase wherever he goes, and he is constantly training other young and older folk who want to follow in his footsteps.

LATIN AMERICAN REVIVAL FIRES BURN ON

Many of the greatest and fastest growing churches in the world are in Latin America. This region of the world has been experiencing revival for several decades.

Church Growth Professor Discovers Major Growth Factor

Dr. C. Peter Wagner, who has succeeded his mentor, Dr. Donald McGavran, as the world's leading expert on church growth, was Professor of Church Growth at Fuller Theological Seminary, School of World Missions, in Pasadena, California. By his own public admission, he had an anti-Pentecostal bias, and found ways to discredit any evidence of the miraculous events which Pentecostals and Charismatics would claim to have experienced or witnessed.

But while doing personal research in South America, to find out what the fastest growing churches had in common, he discovered that virtually all of them had a strong emphasis on signs and wonders and miracles. He began to be more and more convinced that he had been missing an important church growth ingredient.

In 1986, he published, *Spiritual Power and Church Growth* (Creation House), first titled, *Look Out, The Pentecostals Are Coming. (Spreading the Fire by C. Peter Wagner, 1994, Regal Books, A Division of Gospel Light, Ventura, California, U.S.A.)*

Today, Dr. Wagner is a leading teacher on the subject of spiritual gifts, spiritual warfare, and apostolic and prophetic leadership in the church. He is a prolific writer and conference speaker, who brings cutting edge insights to the body of Christ.

Because Dr. Wagner is a man of integrity with an open mind, he not only accepted the obvious fact that the miraculous can help bring people to faith in Jesus, but he embraced those who were leading the way in restoring the miraculous to the church. As a sincere missiologist, he was convinced that joining forces with those who were already successful in winning souls was far more productive than fighting them.

In his very enlightening book, *Churchquake*, Dr. Wagner lists some of the largest of the modern churches and movements, which he calls, "The New Apostolic Churches". Many of these are from South America. All of these churches have a strong belief in the present power of a supernatural God. The following is an excerpt from this significant work:

"The Waves of Love and Peace Church of Buenos Aires, which estimates some 150,000 members, purchased a 2,500 seat theater as its church facility, and five days a week they hold services 18 hours a day. On weekends, they hold services 23 hours a day, closing only from 12 midnight to 1:00 A.M. for cleaning. Just before almost every service, the crowds waiting outside fill the sidewalk and partially block traffic in the street.

"Cesar Castellano's International Charismatic Mission in Bogota, Colombia, finished 1996 having 10,000 home cell groups. His goal for the end of 1997 was 30,000 groups. However, in early 1997, Cesar and his wife, Claudia, were machine-gunned by terrorists bent on killing the pastor of the nation's largest church. Cesar took four bullets and Claudia took three, and they had to spend several months in Houston for treatment. What about the home cell groups? The infrastructure had been so carefully laid that they reached the 30,000 cells they had projected."
(Churchquake, p.48)

Both of these super-sized mega-churches are very strong in their belief that God wants to touch people with His supernatural power. The result of this belief, combined with the other things which are done with excellence, is the phenomenal growth they have experienced.

Argentina's Amazing Revival

When I visited Argentina in 1973 with Elmer Burnette, my spiritual mentor, we found ourselves in a move of God like we had never witnessed in any of our previous ministry trips. As mentioned in an earlier chapter, miracles happened daily for the six weeks we were there. The beneficial side-effects were lavish love, powerful peace and jubilant joy.

But the chief glorious and powerful product of this miraculous display from Heaven was the salvation of over one thousand souls. In addition, thousands of folk, including pastors and other church leaders, began to cry out for the same power of the Holy Spirit in their own lives. Leaders were re-motivated to lead, young people yielded to the call to ministry, and five new churches sprang up, four of them over two hundred strong after only one year. My own life and ministry were also powerfully impacted.

Today, in Argentina, many powerful evangelists and apostolic pastors are continuing to reach and transform whole cities, through the use of God's supernatural power. One well-known evangelist is Carlos Anacondia. A former businessman, Anacondia heard the call to ministry after accepting Christ as Savior. The current revival had its beginning in his crusades in 1982. Twenty years later, these crusades continue to draw huge crowds and feature miracles of healing and deliverance from satanic power.

Annacondia publicly challenges the devil and when the demons manifest, his staff escorts their hosts into another area, where the unclean spirits are evicted from their residence. As in Paul's day, when the unsaved people in the crowds see the power of God in both healing and deliverance, they receive Jesus in huge numbers.

Claudio and Betty Freidzon are the apostolic pastors of King of Kings Church, in Buenos Aires, with a membership that has surged to over 12,000, in 18 years. This is thanks, at least in part, to the continuous explosion of supernatural signs and wonders, and huge crusades that fill the largest stadiums in Buenos Aires.

I had the wonderful privilege recently of attending a camp in Alberta, Canada, where they ministered. The fire of revival and passion for Jesus, accompanied by incredible love, joy and peace spread from them to the large crowds. It was for me an incredible experience and a reminder of the powerful move of God I had experienced 29 years previously.

Along with many others in Argentina, the Friedzons have been used by God to give the people of their nation the opportunity to experience continuous evangelism and growth through the power of a supernatural God, a God who still confirms His Word with signs following. In a country where not long ago, the average church size was 50 people, there are now numerous churches over 7000, with several of these in one city. While the nation continues to struggle with economic issues, the church of Argentina continues to cry out to God for His power to reach the hurting and fearful.

During our visit in 1973, the nation was also going through a crisis time with the re-election of Juan Peron, who had been in exile in Spain. There was much civil unrest and bombs could be heard going off during the night. But the Christians prayed with amazing passion for God's intervention in their nation, and their cries were heard in Heaven.

National crises, as we in North America realize, are times when people think about God and begin to pray, even if they never have before. Argentina still needs the miracle power of God and she now has millions of Christians, who know how to pray and release God's power on the earth.

Ed Silvoso is another Argentine, who has been used to impact and transform whole cities in Argentina. He is taking what he has learned there to the ends of the earth. In the Philippines, he was used to unite the native pastors with the result that salvation came to the man who was the nation's president at the time, as well as his family.

Tommy Hicks Revival

About two decades before Elmer Burnette and I visited Argentina, an awesome thing had taken place that produced a whole new atmosphere for the gospel of Jesus Christ. An American healing evangelist named Tommy Hicks heard God call him to go to Argentina to talk to a man named Peron. Apparently, at the beginning, he didn't know that Juan Peron was the controversial president of Argentina.

Obeying God he flew to Argentina and began to try to make contact with President Peron. Through a series of miraculous events, he met with a close aid or cabinet minister of Peron's. The man had a physical problem, which was healed when Tommy Hicks prayed for him.

Knowing that Juan Peron was afflicted with one side of his face, the politician asked Tommy Hicks if God could heal his president. The door was opened for him to have an audience with Juan Peron, and God performed the healing instantly.

Juan Peron was so excited that he immediately put Tommy Hicks on national radio and television and gave him the use of the nation's largest stadiums. Quickly, people began to fill up the stadiums and tune in to his radio and television programs.

He ended up more than filling up the 180,000 seat Huracan Stadium, the nation's largest. No sporting event, political event, or any other event had ever filled it. But the power of God was so powerfully released in this stadium that the crowds began coming hours before the stadium opened. An English newspaper in Buenos Aires estimated that the crowd totaled an incredible 200,000.[1]

Argentina, like other Latin American countries, had to that time been very anti-protestant, and especially hostile towards evangelicals. But the miracle God did for the president changed everything overnight. Today, Argentina and other Latin American countries are seeing incredible continuous revival, as a result of God's power to perform signs and wonders before the eyes of the people.

SOUTH KOREAN PASTOR LEADS WORLD'S LARGEST CHURCH

Dr. David Yonggi Cho of Seoul, South Korea, with the help of six or seven hundred associate pastors, presides over Yoido Full Gospel Church, a congregation of seven or eight hundred thousand believers. This is by far the largest local church in the history of Christianity. His ministry began only after he discovered the power of God to heal.

With a goal of becoming a great medical doctor, Cho had formerly had little time for spiritual things or religious people, whom he thought were "weak and feeble." But when he found himself dying with tuberculosis, he was introduced to Jesus, and was miraculously healed.

Cho's church had been known for its focus on prayer and the supernatural healing power of God. This focus on a God of power and love has been just what the doctor ordered for the often-oppressed people of South Korea. It has helped bring a sense of security to hundreds of thousands of citizens of Seoul, who live not too many miles from the Demilitarized Zone, which divides Communist North Korea from democratic South Korea. The small Korean Peninsula has for centuries also been subject to aggression from its larger Asian neighbors, especially China and Japan.

Since the Korean war, the South has depended on help from its allies to defend itself from North Korean aggression. At the time of this writing, my wife, Brenda, and I have made two trips to this beautiful place and have fallen in love with its precious and resilient people. We know that they are also a very courageous people, but they are very aware of the fact that they are still vulnerable without outside help. This has aided them to seek their security in God. And thus the churches that demonstrate God's power to do the supernatural have been their top choice.

CHINA'S UNDERGROUND CHURCH GROWS
WITH BIBLICAL PROPORTIONS

Estimates of the number of Christians in China vary, but many project more than one hundred million committed Christians in this oppressive Communist nation. When missionaries were forced out of the country after World War II, there were reportedly only one million Christians. This tremendous growth has happened in the midst of terrible persecution, and in spite of the fact that many pastors and churches have been without any copies of the written Scriptures.

Today, the Christian church continues to explode in China, while the religious oppression continues. I have personally seen video footage, filmed in the 1990's, of Christian gatherings behind the "Bamboo Curtain" that documented the explosive growth of this "Underground Church".

The missionary from Hong Kong, who made the recording, showed huge outdoor crowds in intense prayer and worship, which began early in the morning, and lasted for several hours. People appeared totally lost in the presence of God. Then the video showed us individuals who were known for their miracle ministries, including a man they called Elijah. According to the missionary, this man had seen many incredible miracles take place, including the raising of several people from the dead.

The proliferation of the miraculous in China has more than offset the persecution factor. One of the repeated miracles is the way the communist officials have ignored the huge outdoors crowds in so many cases. Many government officials have also been saved and transformed, becoming allies instead of enemies.

New converts quickly become dedicated evangelists, who believe in the power of God, and expect the same results as the early church in the book of Acts. The result is that people see the miraculous and believe in God, and the church just keeps growing.

Dr. C. Peter Wagner reports the following:

"My friend, David Wang of Asian Outreach, helped me through my paradigm shift in the early 1980's by bringing me firsthand reports of multitudes of simple Chinese people coming to Christ through signs and wonders.

Wang told, for example, of a commune of more than 30,000 that remarkably was all Christian. The commune had become known as 'Yesu Mountain.' The Christian church there for years had been small and struggling, virtually throttled by an aggressive communist party leader from Beijing. Then the communist official developed advanced cancer in his nose that was beyond the scope of medical science. In desperation and in fear of losing his life, he swallowed his pride and asked the Christian leader he had been persecuting to pray to God for healing. The cancer was totally cured, the man became a believer and the way was opened for a people movement that swept the whole commune. The officer was subsequently jailed but rejoiced for the privilege of suffering for Christ, as did many in the book of Acts (see Acts 5:41).

Throughout China today, such stories are almost as common as chopsticks. As a result, at this writing, an estimated 35,000 Chinese are becoming Christians every single day. In sheer magnitude, it dwarfs anything Luke could have possibly imagined.[2]

Another story which has come from China and is being shared by testimony in North American churches is about a young Chinese Christian in his late teens who had been saved for a few months and was now teaching a Sunday School class. He was called on to come to a home where a drunken father had just killed his wife, and was in remorse for what he had done.

When he arrived, the room was filled with village elders, and the mother had been dead for several hours. The little girl, who had heard about Jesus from the young teacher, reminded him about the stories of Jesus, who had been raised from the dead and had raised others from the dead. She asked him to pray for her dead mother.

With no faith and in fear of the village elders, he prayed a quick prayer and tried to leave. The little girl blocked the exit and told him he wasn't finished yet. He went back and prayed again and was again stopped from leaving. When he looked into the eyes of the little girl and saw her radiant faith, he became charged with the zeal of the Lord, and commanded the dead woman to arise.

When she obediently responded, the news spread like wildfire and the whole village was converted. Many reports reveal that praying for the dead is a normal occurrence in certain regions of China. If God does not raise them up, then they accept the idea that perhaps it was their time to go. But many have seen the dead raised.

INSPIRING FAITH IN THE WESTERN WORLD

We have been focusing on some of the "hot spots" of revival and evangelism around the world. All of these seem to be flowing in harmony with the biblical record that signs and wonders are catalysts for producing faith in the unbeliever.

But the western world, including Europe, North America and Australia, has not seen the same level of "power evangelism" as the regions we have already discussed. Many western world Christians have seen very little evidence that signs and wonders have impacted the world to believe in Jesus as Savior and Lord.

Rather, they are much more aware of the results of great evangelists, like Billy Graham, and thousands of other less famous ministries, who simply preach a strong message of salvation, without demonstrating supernatural signs and wonders. They have also seen people come to salvation through aggressive evangelistic programs such as Evangelism Explosion, or other denominational or church-sponsored strategies.

Many non-pentecostal churches also have strong emphases on attracting the sinner, through seeker-friendly services. In their meetings people can invite their neighbors to a very entertaining, but also impacting service. The most famous of these is probably Willow Creek, a mega-church, in the Chicago suburbs, led by Pastor Bill Hybels. This church has brought many believers to Christ without any great emphasis on signs and wonders.

While it may be true that the miraculous is not as predominant in the western world as it is in Africa, Latin America and parts of Asia, there have been, and still are, many powerful moves of God in North America and other regions of the western world. I believe the evidence will show that in the majority of these movements supernatural occurrences have been a major catalyst to evangelism. These movements range from the late nineteenth century healing crusades of Albert Benjamin Simpson, the founder of the Christian and Missionary Alliance, to the modern Houses of Prayer and Healing Rooms that are springing up all over North America and the world.

Founder of Christian and Missionary Alliance Preaches Divine Healing

In the late 1800's A. B. Simpson, a Canadian-born Presbyterian pastor, became persuaded that physical healing was available for every Christian through the atonement of Christ. He began preaching and writing about this truth, until he was conducting large healing crusades in the United States and beyond. Along with this belief, Simpson had a powerful passion for missions and began an organization or "Alliance" to promote foreign missions.

A. B. Simpson did not intend to start another denomination, but desired to create a fellowship to promote missions among churches of all faiths. The important point for this discussion is that through a man who preached and practiced divine healing, multiplied thousands have come to Christ, both in the western world and in scores of nations around the world.

Other Early Healing Evanglists

Two of the most powerful healing evangelists that ministered in the early part of the twentieth century were Smith Wigglesworth and John G. Lake. Wigglesworth was known for his bold and radical faith and vigorous actions in bringing healing to people. At least fourteen cases were documented of the raising of the dead in his ministry, but the actual number may be as high as twenty-three. The results in the salvation of lost souls were corresponding. He could not recall one week when he saw less than fifty souls saved.[3]

John G. Lake pursued the healing power of God, after suffering the loss of several family members to illness and disease. He became a missionary to South Africa and started many churches and a

Pentecostal denomination. Through his message of God's love and power, confirmed by signs following, he established over 600 congregations in only five years. In fact, "Lakes combined work numbered seven hundred thousand members in a nation of fifteen million people. Without a doubt, the incredible miracles were the drawing card to this amazing spiritual rebirth of a nation."[4]

When he returned to the United States, he opened the historical Healing Rooms in Spokane, Washington, and then in Portland, Oregon. These became famous world-wide, and many people found the Lord through his ministry. Today, these healing rooms have been revived, largely through the ministry of Cal Pierce, a "lay" Christian, who was first impacted by renewal in his California church in the mid-nineties, and then directed by the Holy Spirit to move to Spokane. The result was a vision to restore the "wells of healing" and reopen the original healing rooms.

The Explosion of Pentecostalism

Early in the twentieth century in various parts of North America, Christians began to experience the renewal of the phenomenon of "speaking in tongues". The most famous early outpouring of this spiritual gift is known as "The Azuza Street Revival". Christians hungry for more intimacy with God and more power for living the Christian life, began to gather for "tarrying" meetings, praying for an outpouring of the Holy Spirit, as recorded in the book of Acts.

This powerful movement began to explode into every Christian denomination, causing much controversy and debate. While there were surely many problems with attitudes on both sides of the debate, ultimately, those who had experienced this move were either not free to practice it in their churches, or they were asked to leave. As a result, several new denominations were quickly formed, some of which eventually divided over other doctrinal issues.

The Assemblies of God

The largest of these new church organizations was the Assemblies of God, which today is one of the world's largest Christian denominations.

It is also one of the most aggressive in evangelism and missions.

The following is an excerpt from the web site of the Assemblies of God:

"The beginning of the modern Pentecostal revival is generally traced to a prayer meeting at Bethel Bible College in Topeka, Kansas, on January 1, 1901. While many others had spoken in tongues previously during almost every period of spiritual revival, most researchers agree it was here that recipients of the experience, through study of the Scriptures, came to believe speaking in tongues is the biblical evidence for the baptism in the Holy Spirit.

The revival spread rapidly to Missouri and Texas, then to California and elsewhere. A three year revival meeting at Azusa Street Mission in Los Angeles attracted believers from across the nation and overseas and served as a springboard to send the Pentecostal message around the world.

Reports of what was taking place were carried in scores of periodicals and other publications that sprang up with the movement.

Spontaneous revivals also began to break out about that time in other parts of the world and on various mission fields."

Today, this denomination reports the following information on its website:

From the beginning, Assemblies of God ministries have focused on evangelism and missions and have resulted in a continuing growth at home and abroad. Our constituency has climbed from the founding convention attendance of 300 to more than 2.5 million in the United States and over 35 million overseas.

Today, Assemblies of God people worship in over 12,000 churches in the U.S. and in 210,435 churches and outstations in 186 other nations. The aggressive missions programs of the church are designed to establish self-supporting and self-propagating national church bodies in every country. Ministers and leaders are trained in 1,845 foreign Bible schools — more than any other U.S. based denomination. The Assemblies of God has 20 endorsed Bible colleges, liberal arts colleges, and a seminary in the U.S.

Several Assemblies of God churches have had major impact on Christianity around the world. One of these was the already-mentioned church in Seoul, Korea, pastored by David Yonggi Cho. Another great church is in Sydney, Australia, where Hillsongs Music was born. This mega-church has exported an enormous amount of contemporary worship music all around the world.

One of the most world-impacting churches in the past ten years has been the Brownsville Assembly of God Church in Pensacola, Florida. Holding packed-out revival services almost every night of the week for several years, the influence of this one large church has been staggering. For some time, if anyone wanted to get a seat in the auditorium, they would have to stand in line from morning till evening. Many pastors from far and wide brought the revival to their own churches, and the impact of this revival could never be calculated.

The Foursquare Movement

Another significant Pentecostal movement early in the twentieth century was founded by Aimee Semple McPherson, a pioneer of women in public ministry. The following is an excerpt from the website of the Foursquare Church.

"having experienced a profound religious conversion at age seventeen, Aimee began preaching across the United States and later, the world. In 1918, she established her base in Los Angeles, California, where in 1923, the 5,500 seat Angelus Temple was dedicate and became the center of her revival, healing and benevolent ministries.

She was the first woman to receive a FCC radio license and was a pioneer religious broadcaster. Her sermons were the first to incorporate the contemporary communications of that day into her preaching of the Gospel.

193

From Angelus Temple she performed an extensive social ministry, providing hot meals for more than 1.5 million people during the Great Depression. She summarized her message into four major points known as "The Foursquare Gospel," and founded a denomination called The International Church of the Foursquare Gospel.

From its beginning at Angelus Temple, the International Church of the Foursquare Gospel has now grown to include more than 1,900 churches in the United States and Canada, and over 24,000 churches worldwide. There are currently more than 2.8 million members in 99 countries around the globe. It presently ranks as one of the three or four most distinguished branches of Pentecostalism. Aimee Semple McPherson died in 1944, while conducting a crusade in Oakland, California.

The total evangelistic impact of all the various Pentecostal churches in the past 100 years would be impossible to calculate. Although many "Pentecostal" or "Full Gospel" churches do not regularly experience a great abundance of supernatural phenomena, their formation and growth was based on a belief and an experience that was very dependent on a God of signs and wonders. Speaking in tongues, for instance, was almost always considered a "sign" that the Holy Spirit had been poured out.

The Healing Movement of the Mid-Twentieth Century

In 1948, while Israel was officially becoming a nation, the church, began to experience new power. At the same time that natural Israel was being restored to its natural possessions, spiritual Israel was being restored to its spiritual possessions.

In the Evangelical/Fundamentalist camp, great things were happening. Youth For Christ became a powerful tool for evangelism. A young preacher named Billy Graham began as one of their youth speakers, and quickly became a nationally-known evangelist, bringing thousands to Christ in massive crusades.

In the Pentecostal camp, healing crusades began to explode with a wide variety of healing evangelists. Oral Roberts, who himself was healed of tuberculosis and stuttering, claimed that God had called him to bring His healing power to the world. William Branham ministered with an incredibly accurate gift of knowledge, identifying the infirmity and other information of each person in the healing line. I personally witnessed his ministry as a young person growing up in Saskatchewan, Canada.

Others quickly joined the movement. These included A. A. Allen, T. L. Osborn, Gordon Lindsay, Jack Coe, William Freeman, David Nunn, and others. Many of these joined together to form a loose fellowship. Gordon Lindsay was clearly the leader in bringing them together. He published a magazine called, "The Voice of Healing", which quickly became very influential and a powerful tool to publicize the healing ministry in America and around the world.

Kathryn Kuhlman was another well-known healing evangelist, who came on the scene about the same time. She never became a part of the "Voice of Healing" fellowship, but she did use the power of the miraculous to draw great crowds. She would then teach them about the Holy Spirit and the miracle of salvation, with significant results.

Some of these ministries had huge tent meetings or coliseum crusades. Testimonies of healings were given frequently to encourage faith in others, who still needed a miracle. As always, when unusual things are reportedly taking place, many people come just out of curiosity, or just to see a good show. Many of the curious and former skeptics find faith for salvation in a powerful God who can save as well as heal.

It should be made clear at this point that a number of the big names in the healing ministry did not handle their fame and popularity well. One of these insisted on going beyond his gifting and tried to become a teacher/theologian. He ended up espousing some very strange and divisive doctrines, which exalted himself above other evangelists. He was taken from this world before he reached old age.

Another man with a great miracle ministry may have died an alcoholic, according to many reports. Others may have used their influence to accumulate great wealth. While being blessed with great wealth is certainly not a sin, it should not be at the expense of those who sacrificed their limited resources thinking that their offering was going to build the Kingdom of God.

But others, kept their reputation pure and worked hard and unselfishly to build for Jesus. One such man was Gordon Lindsay, who with his wife Freda, served God faithfully for many years. With a great burden for evangelism and missions, the Lindsays established a training center for young people in Dallas, Texas, which they called Christ For the Nations Institute.

C.F.N.I.

Today, the Dallas campus houses about 2000 students from around the world. Most of these make extensive missions trips during their two or three year stints at the college. In addition, other campuses have been opened in other nations to make the training more accessible to non-Americans. Since her husband's death, Freda has carried on the ministry and taken it to new heights.

Evangelism is still a major emphasis at CFNI, and Freda Lindsay is a strong believer in the thesis that the best way to win souls is to show people the miraculous power of God, just as Jesus and the apostles had. It had worked well for the Lindsays during their ministry together, and they had seen it work well for others as well.

In addition, students are encouraged to seek God for a supernatural ministry for the sake of bringing others to faith in God. To facilitate this, a variety of speakers are brought in to share their own testimonies, and motivate the students to a higher level of ministry. Their testimonies often include the signs and wonders that they have witnessed in their own lives and ministries.

Some Christian leaders believe that God lifted the strong healing anointing of the mid-1900's, because so many of its recipients were guilty of abusing this gift from God. Many do affirm, however, that this anointing is being restored, and that the church has matured enough at this point to be much wiser in handling this source of power. Instead of building personal empires, leaders in the body of Jesus are becoming more committed to the Kingdom of God.

JESUS PEOPLE AND THE CHARISMATIC MOVEMENT

By the end of the sixties, two interrelated movements were taking place in America and many other parts of the world. The Charismatic movement had begun. This was another wave of Pentecostalism, which began to re-invade the older and non-pentecostal churches. This movement exploded with an excitement about the power of the Holy Spirit, including signs and wonders, especially the gift of tongues, and the laying on of hands for healing.

No denominations were immune. From formal "high-church" Roman Catholics and Episcopalians, to Baptists and Nazarenes, prayer groups were springing up, bringing a brand new excitement to their churches. Many of these could not remember any kind of real or freely-expressed excitement in their Christianity before.

One well-known case is that of Father Dennis Bennett of St. Luke's Episcopal Church in Seattle, Washington. He had a profound experience with the Lord and began to share it with his church. While continuing to serve the people in their formal services in a manner with which they were accustomed, he added special prayer meetings. People could come and receive prayer for healing, and/or pray for the baptism of the Holy Spirit.

Some Charismatics, like Father Bennett were accepted by their denominations and fellowships, while others were not. But whether they stayed or felt compelled to leave, they carried with them an excitement about the power of God that could not be shaken.

The zeal of these folks began to spread outside the walls of the church. Soon they began to affect the hippie culture, which had been popular during the 1960's. Disillusioned youth had rejected what they considered the hypocrisy of "the establishment", and found alternative life-styles. They were trying drugs of all kinds, fostering what they called "free love", and wearing shabby clothes, while refusing to get hair cuts or take baths.

This sub-culture in America was looking for something different and exciting. The Charismatics had it and were more than willing to share it with them. The result was, at least in part, the "Jesus People" movement.

I was personally introduced to a group of these young radicals in Canada in the summer of 1969. One young man, who was seeking reality in the wrong way, had actually encountered God while high on LSD. He was powerfully changed and began to witness to others. By the time I met him he had already led over two hundred people to Jesus, most of whom were university students at the University of Saskatchewan, Regina Campus, where I was attending at the time.

I began joining his group for early morning prayer meetings. These college-age young people would sit in a circle and sing, *"We are One in the Spirit, We are One in the Lord."* They would read Scripture and pray in English and as well as in tongues. Some would exercise the gift of prophecy, even though their knowledge of how to use their gifts was very primitive.

The important point however, was that they were attracted to Christianity, not because a religious or formal organization appealed to them, or reason or logic convinced them, but rather, they were attracted to Christianity because they found other Christian people who were excited about a supernatural experience and relationship with God. While the influence of supernatural signs and wonders probably varied with different Jesus People groups, there was certainly a significant interaction between these two groups.

Calvary Chapel

Many traditional churches were not eager to welcome the hippie-type church-goers, who were beginning to invade their sanctuaries on Sunday mornings and evenings. A man named Chuck Smith took a totally different approach. Recognizing the potential harvest among the hippie generation, he began holding services geared specifically for them.

Outdoor concerts with a youthful music style were the norm for this movement, and young people, as well as some of the older generation, began to fill their meetings. The Calvary Chapel Movement grew and continues to flourish, although it has changed with the times to remain relevant in a changing world.

Youth With A Mission (YWAM)

Another powerful evangelistic and missionary force that grew out of a Pentecostal movement was Youth With a Mission, founded by Lorne Cunningham. One of many youth missions organizations, including Operation Mobilization, and the Navigators, YWAM is now one of the largest interdenominational ministries in the world staffed by 12,000 volunteers in 800 bases in 135 countries.

Founding in 1960, YWAM has focused on discipleship to prepare young and old alike for the rigors of missionary evangelism. Thousands of people have taken the Discipleship Training School (DTS). I know of several, whose lives have been radically impacted by this training.

The results, in terms of the number of converts of this ministry, could never be calculated. So many volunteers are working in so many places impacting both the non-Christian natives and the Christian leaders and workers on the mission fields as well as in the "homeland". But we know that the results are highly significant, and we know that YWAM has always had a belief in calling on God to do the supernatural.

Christian Television Takes Off

Before and shortly after the beginning of the 1970's, many new ministries were being launched. The Christian School movement was quickly followed by the Home School movement. Bill Gothard's "Institute in Basic Youth Conflicts" began to fill large stadiums for week-long seminars. Many other movements were taking off at the same time, but one of the most impacting was the launching of Christian television networks.

CBN

Pat Robertson, the son of a former U.S. senator, who ran a

significant U.S. presidential campaign in 1992, was the trailblazer in Christian television with the birthing of CBN, the Christian Broadcasting Network. CBN was actually first formed in 1960. The first broadcast was October 1, 1961. The 700 Club, initiated in 1964, was a new approach to Christian programming, with news, interviews, testimonies and prayer for the people.

But what may have been the most interesting to many viewers was the public broadcasting of words of knowledge for people who needed healing or other miracles in their lives. The first time I saw the program, I was amazed at the words that were being given to people in the TV audience.

I had heard hundreds of similar words in my travels with E. R. Burnette, my mentor and spiritual father, but I had never seen anything like this on television. This was one of the first opportunities for non-Pentecostals to witness this and other elements of the supernatural, without going to a Pentecostal meeting.

Today CBN has an expanded world-wide ministry with tremendous impact. Operation Blessings provides all kinds of practical and financial assistance to needy people all around the world. Regent University is an outstanding academic institution that equips thousands of students in many fields, including law and communications. Their legal department, called the American Center for Law and Justice (ACLJ) under the very gifted leadership of Jay Seculow has championed Christian causes before the United States Supreme Court.

Another very important part of CBN's ministry has been the prayer and counseling ministry. While the 700 Club program is airing, people are given phone numbers to call to receive salvation or counseling. Over the years, many thousands of folk have called and prayed a salvation prayer over the phone.

TBN

In 1973 Paul and Jan Crouch launched what is today the world's largest Christian television network, the Trinity Broadcasting Network (TBN). Today, the ministry is continuously growing, with their "Praise

The Lord" program seen daily on about 3600 television stations at the time of this writing. They are broadcasting on 23 satellites, the internet and thousands of cable systems around the world.

Another powerful outreach of TBN is the development of their movie making division. Movies such as "The Omega Code", "The Champion" and "Miggedo" have played to large public theater audiences across America and the world.

TBN is another modern ministry, which makes use of the power of signs and wonders to bring the gospel to North America and the nations. Most of the guests and speakers proclaim and/or demonstrate the supernatural power of God on the various programs.

Like CBN, TBN offers prayer and counseling for their viewers, and multiplied thousands have called in and given their lives to God. It would be safe to say that there are few ministries today that touch as many individuals as TBN.

Benny Hinn

Although the healing movement of the mid-century did not keep up the momentum it had seen in its prime, there have always been healing evangelists who continued to see God do the miraculous in their meetings. Katheryn Kuhlmann was a notable example. One man who served under her ministry was Benny Hinn. As a young man, he caught the vision of bringing God's healing power to people in need.

Today, Benny Hinn's ministry includes a daily television program, monthly crusades in North America and frequent overseas campaigns. But although most people think of him as a healing evangelist, he has seen incredible results in bringing people to faith for salvation.

In a recent Las Vegas, Nevada crusade I was rather surprised to see over 2000 people per night walk forward to receive Jesus as Savior, even before the sick were prayed for. The atmosphere of worship and the expectancy of the people released a desire to make "Jesus the healer" to also become "Jesus the Savior".

In overseas crusades the crowds are often many times larger than the American crusades, and the response to the salvation invitation is also far greater. No matter how many critics attack his ministry, people continuously pack out every crusade, both at home and abroad, and few would deny that the results are impressive and enriching the Kingdom of God.

In a recent crusade in Honduras, the crowd numbered about one hundred thousand, according to the local officials. Twenty thousand of these prayed the salvation prayer with Benny Hinn.

Another strong positive aspect of Benny Hinn's ministry is the force he has become for unity in the body of Christ. He has broadened significantly his circle of influence by bringing a variety of ministries onto his daily television program, "This is Your Day", seen now in 190 nations. Because unity is so critical to releasing God's power and producing faith in the unbeliever, this is a very positive and significant trend.

The Vineyard Phenomenon

One of the largest and fastest growing Christian movements in the past thirty years is the Vineyard. This movement, begun by founder, John Wimber, was built with a strong focus on signs and wonders in the church. The first time I heard about the Vineyard, a pastor friend told me about a seminar he was attending on signs and wonders, conducted by John Wimber.

Since then Vineyard churches have sprung up in most American cities. At present, they have over 500 churches in the United States alone, and are in over 70 nations as well. Some of these churches have grown quite large and have had a major impact on the Christian world.

Toronto

One of these was the Toronto Airport Vineyard, pastored by John Arnott. In 1994 a powerful, and controversial revival broke out, when a Vineyard pastor, named Randy Clark, from St. Louis, came for special meetings. This revival, which quickly took the church from a 400 seat auditorium to a 4000 seat facility, continues to bring thousands of visitors from around the world.

These visitors, many of them pastors, have been taking this unusual revival back to their churches and their nations. Because of the controversial nature of this revival, the relationship between Toronto and the Vineyard headquarters in Anaheim, California, became severely strained. Eventually their relationship was severed and the church was renamed, the Toronto Airport Christian Fellowship.

Kansas City

Another powerful church, which was affiliated with the Vineyard for a time, was the Metro Vineyard Fellowship of Kansas City, pastored then by Mike Bickle. This church has also impacted Christianity by taking a leading role in the restoration of prophetic ministry to the church. Well-known prophets, such as Paul Cain, and Bob Jones, demonstrated to many how powerful the gift of prophecy could be in raising the faith level of individuals who were given prophetic words.

Although John Wimber passed away in the late nineties, and the movement underwent some changes, there is no doubt that through the Vineyard many people were brought into the Kingdom of God. And in addition to the many conversions because of the focus on and production of healings, signs and wonders, many who were already Christians had their faith in God strengthened.

Prophetic Evangelism

Jesus demonstrated the power of prophetic evangelism in John 1 and 4. Nathaniel, the skeptic, and the Samaritan woman both were convinced and affected others because they received a prophetic word of knowledge. But these things still happen today, and the results can be awesome. In fact, I believe that along with seeking for the visible signs and wonders, we should strongly desire to develop the prophetic gifts for the purpose of evangelism. This was clearly Paul's desire as revealed in I Corinthians 14.

In prophetic classes we heard from a man with a prophetic ministry, who told of the days when he would go to a restaurant and not be able to eat because he would get words for total strangers who were eating their meal. He would walk over and begin to reveal their hearts to them. They would begin to cry and then he would immediately lead them to the Lord. His wife got tired of going to restaurants with him and eating alone, although she rejoiced in the results.

In our own experience, we have seen some results with prophetic evangelism, although most of it has been in church or house meetings. We saw a small group of young adults accept the love of the Lord in a basement meeting in Calgary, Canada. The result was that several more people came to the Lord and many of them have become faithful in a local church. Through prophetic words of knowledge, several have been released from suicidal thoughts or plans and have received the assurance of God's love. My wife, Brenda, has also given words to many total strangers, who were presented in a personal way with the love of Jesus. Most of them received it gladly.

One of the most exciting reports we have heard in recent days was from a young prophet, named Shawn Boltz, from Kansas City. As a child, the prophetic gifting was being activated and as a teen-ager, he became a youth leader in his church in Sacramento, California.

As a youth leader, he and others trained their teens in prophetic evangelism. During the time of his ministry there, he reports that about two thousand souls were saved through that ministry on the streets of Sacramento.

THE EVANGELISTIC IMPACT OF NON-PENTECOSTAL MOVEMENTS

SEEKER-FRIENDLY CHURCHES

In an effort to reach out to the non-churched, many evangelical groups in the past several decades have purposefully shifted from the traditional church service style to a format which is much less threatening to one who is not yet a believer, or to put it into their own terms, one who is a "seeker." Their services are usually very entertaining and feature speakers who are well-known in the secular field.

They focus the message on issues that relate to believers and non-believers alike. There may be small group meetings during the week, as well as a corporate week-night gathering for deeper ministry, but the main weekend services are designed to reveal the relevance of the gospel to everyday living, and the blessings of a relationship with Jesus.

Two of the most famous seeker-friendly churches are the Crystal Cathedral in Southern California, and Willow Creek Community Church in Barrington, Illinois, a suburb of Chicago. Both have impacted hundreds of thousands of lives in positive ways. I had the privilege recently of visiting the latter.

Willow Creek Community Church

Anyone who takes in a service at "Willow" can't help but be impressed with a number of things that make it special. Everything done there speaks "Excellence". The facility is a sharp-looking structure that is both beautiful and practical. The children's ministries, youth ministries and so many other ministries are the very finest available, utilizing great creativity as well as apparently plentiful resources.

But the captivating aspects for me were the various parts of the Sunday morning service that flowed with grace and power. The congregational singing was very brief, but powerfully led and impacting. There was a dramatic testimony of a lady who had recovered from years of alcoholism, through relationships within the church, and then a high quality drama, which used humor, but made a strong point, to challenge the seekers to think about their life-style.

Following a touching special number, Pastor Bill Hybels took the microphone and shared in a down-to-earth and humorous style a very impacting message. It was something that any Christian or non-Christian could learn from. At the end of the message, a very gracious invitation was made to all who might be seekers in the house, and a sincere salvation prayer was offered for all who desired to make a life-changing decision for Christ.

I had the privilege of interacting with several leaders of the church's drama and prayer teams and was impressed with their dedication and desire to serve God with all their hearts. I was informed by one of the members who worked with the outreach and evangelism force that in the previous year (2001), a total of one thousand, one hundred people had made decisions for Christ. The goal had been some-what higher, but they were grateful for the harvest which had come in.

Although many Christians criticize the seeker-friendly format for various reasons, I believe that Pastor Hybels and others like him are faithfully doing what they have been called to do. Certainly, most of their critics have not accomplished a fraction of what some of these ministries have produced.

The fact is, we can all learn from each other. There are those of us in the Pentecostal/Charismatic camp that claim to believe in things that we haven't ever experienced or practiced in our church life. And yet we have developed a "Superiority Complex" over those who don't have our theology, but are just as successful, or even more so than we are at winning souls.

In our arrogance, we have ignored the values of the other camp that have made some of them quite effective. One of the values I discovered at Willow Creek was a focus on simplicity with sincerity, which meant a noticeable absence of hype, especially in the area of pumping visitors for finances. Instead visitors at Willow Creek were asked to just let the offering basket pass by them. Another value was the sincere concern for the individual and the clear message that there were many other churches that they could recommend, if Willow Creek was not their preferred style.

Billy Graham Evangelistic Association

The ministry of Dr. Billy Graham was launched into the public eye at a 1949 Los Angeles crusade. According to the association's web-site, Dr. Graham has preached to more people in live audiences that anyone else in history. They report that he has ministered live to more than 210 million people in more than 185 countries and territories. In addition, his films, videos and television programs have reached millions more.

The films alone have been translated into forty languages and viewed by more than 250 million people. Although other evangelical, non-Pentecostal evangelists have been on the scene during the same half-century, there have not been any that have rivaled his popularity and success in bringing people to faith in Jesus Christ.

Dr. Graham's message was always simple, but relevant. The only miracle he offered to people was the miracle of a changed life. For millions of people, that was enough.

There were of course, plenty of references to the miracles involving Jesus on the earth, including the miracle of His resurrection. But people were never invited to come for physical healing or other needs that would require the supernatural power of God, other than salvation. What Dr. Graham did so well was what he was called by God to do. He was called to present the message of salvation to those who were willing and ready to hear it.

Personally, I am extremely grateful to the ministry of Billy Graham. It was while watching him on T.V. that my wife, Brenda, reached out to Jesus for her own salvation. She was a young teen, and had already lived through a lot of emotional pain, when a visiting aunt turned on the "Hour of Decision". Her spirit was stirred by the message and the invitation and she accepted the invitation to bring Jesus into her life and her world. After that, Jesus was always there for her, no matter what was happening in her world.

Many have criticized Dr. Graham's ministry, saying that only a small percentage of converts from Billy Graham crusades continue to live a Christian life-style. But the same thing could probably be said of many other soul-winning efforts. Of course, it is important to follow-up people who make decisions, which the Association works hard to do, but I do know that there have been millions who have gone on to live for Jesus, including my wife.

If one tried to calculate the results of this one ministry as it continues to reproduce results, it would be an impossible task. My wife alone, has touched several thousands of people, just in the last few years, with personal words of encouragement. A good number of individuals have found Jesus as a result of her ministry, and I know that many more will in the future. Those she encourages also become more active in reaching others for Jesus, and so the fruit continues to keep on growing.

As one who grew up in the Pentecostal/Charismatic camp, I say thank-you to Billy Graham and all his crew for doing so well what God called them to do. And I apologize for those from our camp who have criticized such an amazing work of God's grace.

Evangelism Explosion

Evangelism Explosion, was founded by Dr. James Kennedy of Coral Ridge Presbyterian Church, in Coral Ridge, Florida, in the early 1960's. It is another very active and effective evangelistic force in the Kingdom of God. Today, according to their web-site, E. E. International is in all 212 nations and 15 territories of the world. Their work is done largely through training church leaders in week-long leadership clinics, which empower churches to run their Evangelism Explosion programs.

The first clinic was held in 1965. Thirty years later, 278 clinics were held, which were attended by 5,534 clinicians. Almost 9,000 professions of faith were made during the on-the-job training, which is an integral part of every clinic.

Of course, these numbers are the results of the training sessions only. The results of the thousands of church ministries using the E. E. program would no doubt be much greater.

The Jesus Film Project

Few international ministry efforts have been rewarded with the phenomenal results attained by the Jesus Film project. Conceived of way back in 1950 by Dr. Bill Bright, founder of Campus Crusade for Christ, the Jesus Film was produced in 1978, with a price-tag of six million U. S. dollars.

The movie, based entirely on Luke's gospel, is very faithful to the biblical text, with many direct quotes in the actual script. It opened in 1979 in 2000 theatres, playing to millions of North Americans, and soon was being carried around the world. The following is an excerpt from the Jesus Film Projects web-site.

"Every two seconds—sometimes in the midst of global chaos and conflict—someone indicates a decision to receive Christ as personal Savior as a result of seeing the "JESUS" film.

Through use by The JESUS Film Project, and more than 1,500 Christian agencies, **this powerful film has been seen by more than 4 billion people worldwide**. On top of that, the great majority of those heard the story of Jesus in a language they easily understand.

As a result, **more than 153 million people have indicated decisions to accept Christ as their personal Savior and Lord.**

The JESUS Film Project seeks to give everyone in the world one chance to hear the gospel in their own language. So whether a person speaks Swahili, French, or a language whose name is extremely difficult for most to pronounce, he or she will encounter the life and message of Jesus in a language "of the heart."

Many mission experts have acclaimed the "JESUS" film as one of the greatest evangelistic success stories of all time. The ultimate success of this project won't be measured by how many people have already seen it, but by how many will follow Him after seeing this film."

The incredible results of this powerful outreach demand that we ask the relevant question to the purpose and thesis of this book. Are all these conversions the result of simply presenting the gospel, or do signs and wonders play a significant role in their conversion?

The Jesus Film is simply and basically the gospel portrayed on screen. It depicts many incredible miracles recorded by Luke, and finishes with the story of the resurrection. Although the viewers may not see a live miracle or sign done before their eyes, the majority of viewers who have accepted Christ are in third-world countries, where films are not nearly as common as they are in the western world.

My personal opinion is that the presentation of the gospel through drama in this film comes across to the native viewer as if he is actually seeing the event live. Thus, the influence of the miracles he sees on the screen has a powerful impact in bringing him to faith in Jesus.

Again, we see a beautiful combination of the pursuit of excellence in presenting the gospel, with the powerful impact of signs and wonders. The result is the maximum number of conversions in a given setting.

Campus Crusade For Christ

In 1951, Dr. Bill and Vonette Bright founded a ministry mainly for the evangelization of students on the college and university campuses of America and the world. The following is information provided by their web-site.

"Campus Crusade for Christ was founded by Bill and Vonette Bright at UCLA in 1951. One year later, Bill Bright wrote The Four Spiritual Laws - likely the most widely distributed religious booklet in history, with approximately 2.5 billion printed to date.

By 1960, Campus Crusade was established on 40 campuses in the United States and in two other countries. During the 1960's the ministry began conducting international Christmas conferences and summer mission projects.

In 1983, a major event called KC'83 was held in Kansas City that drew 17,000 college students. Almost a decade later, in 1991, Campus Crusade relocated its headquarters from California to Orlando, FL.

US News & World Report rated Campus Crusade as the top religious charity in the United States in 1995. Money magazine ranked the ministry as the most "efficient" religious ministry in the U.S. in 1996.

By the year 2000, Campus Crusade for Christ International, the parent organization for the college ministry, had more than 24,000 full time staff members, and more than 500,000 trained volunteers serving in 191 countries. Founder Bill Bright passed the leadership torch to new president Steve Douglass, formerly executive vice-president and director of U.S. Ministries in 2001.

In 2002, the campus ministry of Campus Crusade for Christ currently has active movements on more than 1,130 campuses with 45,000 students involved. There are 1,800 full-time campus ministry staff members serving in the U.S. and internationally. The ministry is sharing the gospel with approximately 9 million students each year with 6,000 recorded decisions by students to accept Christ last year."

SUMMING UP THIS CHAPTER

There are certainly many more movements from both camps that we could highlight in this study, but from the information already gathered it is more than obvious that there has been powerful fruit from a wide variety of movements and Christian organizations who have had a love for evangelism. But what we would like to emphasize here is the fact that although there have been some great evangelistic efforts from ministries of both Christian camps, we are still not getting the job done.

The majority of the masses of North America and the rest of the world still don't live for Jesus. With all we have done, there is still so much more to do, and the enemy and our pride have kept us from working together in unity to bring in the harvest with maximum efficiency.

We must come to a place of understanding that we all can learn some of the secrets of successful evangelism from each other. All it takes is humbling ourselves to listen to and study each other's successes with open hearts and minds. C. Peter Wagner was able to recognize the power of the miraculous to bring people into the Kingdom of God. But we all need to be open to each other in both camps, because God didn't give the whole puzzle to any one group.

God gave each of us a number of pieces to the puzzle, but if we try to make the whole picture with just our pieces, we will never see what God wants us to see. It's only when we put our pieces together and let God show us how they fit, that we will see the masterpiece God has in mind.

The potential for reaching the world for Jesus is truly incredible. **But realizing that potential requires that we get together and join forces for the Kingdom of God.**

It is undeniable that the power of the supernatural is a very potent force for winning souls. We must not forget what is happening in so many nations of the world through the outreach of miracle crusades. At the same time, we must acknowledge that some very good results have come as a result of the pursuit of excellence, diligent preparation, and a loving and sincere presentation of the gospel.

Would it not be great if we could first of all just acknowledge that the other camp is making a solid contribution to the cause of the Kingdom of God, and encourage them to keep up the good work?

And secondly, would it not be even greater if we could learn from the other camp and employ a combination of the most successful strategies of both camps.

The exciting thing to report is that we are seeing this very thing beginning to come to pass in some powerful ways. Various Christian television programs have been highlighting this trend by bringing together leaders from many different streams of Christianity. Numerous non-Pentecostal leaders have been invited to speak on programs hosted by Pentecostals. Evangelicals have welcomed to their programs and churches Christian leaders and authors from the Charismatic or Pentecostal camps.

As this trend picks up steam, as I believe it will, we will see the power of unity released. I personally believe that in most cases we will not have to convince non-Pentecostals that miracles are still for today. They will be experiencing them frequently in their own lives and ministries. It may take crises in our churches or in our society, such as the 9/11 disaster, but our need for God will produce a deep and strong cry for God's intervention and deliverance. It will be a united crying out to God, which will result in God showing His power to whoever calls on His name.

The result will be an excitement about God and His awesome love and power. This in turn will make evangelists out of many, who will take this love and power to the lost.

CHAPTER 15

Signs of the Times

MODERN WONDERS

As we discussed early in this book, wonders are designed to get people's attention, to make them wonder what is going on. All over the world a multitude of signs and wonders are occurring. Some of these are very common in many circles. These include such things as falling under the power of the Holy Spirit, hilarious laughter, shaking, and the appearance of gold dust and other substances.

It should be made clear that many of these experiences have happened in previous revivals throughout history, including The Great Awakening. Some reference was made to this in a previous chapter. I do also believe that most of these could be considered signs, as well as wonders, and therefore we need to ask what kind of a message they are to bring to the church.

Many people argue that these signs and wonders are not of God. Their logic is that if there were no exact examples in Scripture, then the experience is unbiblical or invalid. While there are some experiences in Scripture that are similar to some of these, none of them are exactly like what the church has been experiencing. But frankly, I don't believe the Holy Spirit is limited to doing "carbon copy" signs and wonders.

In the first place, there are many signs and wonders that occurred only once in Scripture. These include most of the plagues of Egypt, the budding of Aaron's rod, making an ax-head float, turning water into wine and walking on water. These were each different than any previous miracle. God is infinitely creative and will not put Himself in any of our "boxes" which we create for Him.

In addition, there are several references to "many signs and wonders", where we are given no idea as to what these signs and wonders were. John writes:

"And truly Jesus did many other signs in the presence of His disciples, which are not written in this book; but these are written that you may believe that Jesus is the Christ, the Son of God, and that believing you may have life in His name." *(John 20:30,31)*

Notice John's purpose for writing about the signs. He recorded the signs so that we will believe. It is still the reason we should demonstrate signs and wonders to the world. We want them to believe.

But the point we are making here is that there were many signs and wonders which were not recorded, both in the ministry of Jesus and in the ministry of the early church. Luke reports the following about the early church:

"Then fear came upon every soul, and many wonders and signs were done through the apostles." *(Acts 2:43)*

"And Stephen, full of faith and power, did great wonders and signs among the people." *(Acts 6:8)*

In these examples and others, we are given no information as to what kind of signs and wonders were done. Knowing God's creativity, many of them could have been different from those we have read about. So if God wants to show His power and get people's attention by knocking them down, or making them shake, He has that privilege, and doesn't need our permission or approval.

I understand people having problems accepting such phenomena, which seem totally strange to them. People react negatively for two reasons. One reason is that they are offended by the person, or by the personality or the "flesh" of the ministries, whom they have seen performing these signs. It is unfortunate, but flesh always seems to manifest when God's power begins to manifest. The flesh is always around where people are around, but it finds greater opportunity to exhibit itself when God's power gets people's attention.

The second reason people have problems with things like falling under the power of God is that we all have our own frame of reference for "normal" Christianity. Whatever our particular tradition happens to be is "normal" to us, even if it is not totally biblical.

For instance, we have many things in most of our churches that have no biblical basis, but we see no problem with them. Let me list a few of them.

1. Of the five ministries mentioned in Ephesians 4:11, we have clear examples of all five except for the pastor. No one in the New Testament is called "Pastor So-and-so". But it is the most common title in our contemporary churches. Apostles and prophets are the most commonly mentioned in Scripture, but the least mentioned in our churches.

2. We read nothing in the Bible about Sunday School, Youth ministry or Women's ministries, but we accept these as normal.

3. Most of our church governments have little biblical basis. Nowhere in Scripture do we read about people voting on a church leader, or voting on anything for that matter, but many Christians have no problem with that practice, thinking the church to be a democracy.

4. Church building programs are never mentioned in the New Testament, but what would we do without them today?

5. Pulpits and wooden crosses are common fixtures in our churches, but we have no evidence that they were in any New Testament church.

At the same time, we read of many things that the early church possessed that we rarely see in our churches today. I believe we should be more concerned about the absence of the possessions of the early church than about the things for which we can't find an exact copy in Scripture.

EARLY CHURCH POSSESSIONS OFTEN LACKING TODAY

1. Unity

One of those "things", which the early church had, was unity. Luke tells us five times in the first five chapters of the book of Acts, the fifth New Testament book, that "They were all in one accord." They had a powerful unity. Amazingly enough, Jesus had prayed five times in John 17, His last prayer before the cross, that they would all be one. Later, divisions in some of the churches brought rebukes from the Apostle Paul. But the early Jerusalem church that revealed the power of God in such an awesome way, was powered by divine unity and the joy and love that came with it.

How do our churches today compare to the standards set by the early Jerusalem church? Do we get as concerned about our lack of unity as we do when something unusual to our traditions occurs in our churches.

2. Power

The early Jerusalem church was a virtual Holy Spirit powerhouse. There were so many signs and wonders that most of them are not recorded in any detail. The supernatural became the natural and the unusual became the usual. The result was a church that grew exponentially. Today, most of our churches grow fractionally, if at all. But there are few who cry out that what we are experiencing is unscriptural.

3. Love

Many believers like to talk about love and proclaim that it is more important than spiritual gifts. But my personal experience is that when true spiritual gifts are flourishing, the love of God is much more abundant and profound than when spiritual gifts are absent. I clearly observed this to be true in Argentina, when the love of the people was so thick that you could practically feel it, see it, and taste it.

At the same time, I find that many people, who argue against the need for gifts, and proclaim that love is more important, are themselves not very loving, especially to those who don't agree with their doctrines. There is such a need in the body of Christ to demonstrate love rather than just talk about it.

The early church was such an awesome example of this. There is no mention of the word "love" in the book of Acts, but we read that the people had a level of unselfishness that we seldom see in our western Christian churches. They were spending a lot of time together and yet they were still in unity.

They were so excited about what God was doing that they were willing to sacrifice their natural possessions for each other. Perhaps Christians should be more concerned with the absence of such things that are so rare in the church today, than with the special signs and wonders that we may not yet understand.

Let's look at one more Scripture here to make the point.

"How is it then, brethren? Whenever you come together, each of you has a psalm, has a teaching, has a tongue, has a revelation, has an interpretation. Let all things be done for edification." (I. Corinthians 14:26)

Paul gave us a sample of what a New Testament service should be like. Obviously, they didn't have bulletins, because they couldn't predict who would give the various words or sing a psalm or teach, or speak in tongues or interpret the tongues. I certainly am not condemning the way we run services today, but we certainly can't prove that our services were modeled in the Bible. Even so many other things happening that are strange to us today, are probably more biblical than what we consider normal.

CONTEMPORARY SIGNS AND WONDERS

Many Christians believe that many of the signs and wonders taking place in Christian circles today are things that have never happened before, or at least not since the early apostolic church. The truth is that most, if not all, of the recent occurrences have been experienced by many in church history, especially during times of revival.

Records from the First and Second Great Awakenings reveal a variety of unusual things taking place. Randy Clark declares, *"These two awakenings both showcased power encounters such as falling, shaking, groaning, shouting, deliverance from demons and falling into trances. These displays of the power of God were also evidenced within the lives of the early Methodist circuit riders, as well as great revivalists such as Charles Grandison Finney.*[8]

Other records show other time periods in church history which produced unusual phenomena in times of special moves of God. It might be an interesting study to investigate whether any significant move of God happened in Christendom where there were no unusual signs and wonders reported. My suspicion is that when there are few evidences of the supernatural or strange occurrences in the church, there is also not much happening in the realm of revival of the church or in the field of evangelism and soul-winning.

Falling Under the Power of the Holy Spirit

Many thousands of people have experienced the power of the Holy Spirit in a way which causes them to fall to the floor. Sometimes they find themselves overcome by the presence of God and have intimate encounters during this time. Other times, they simply lay on the floor in worship or intercession.

The intensity of the experience varies from person to person and ministry to ministry, and some people may fall on purpose, but we have seen and experienced enough of this phenomenon to know that it can be very real. We have seen people lay on the floor for hours. Some have tried to get up without being able to. Others had been in deep intercession and spiritual warfare.

In our own ministry, we don't see many people "go down" under the power of the Holy Spirit, but there have been a number of "surprises". Usually those who do go down are people who are very sensitive to the moving of the Holy Spirit, and they just "crumble" when we lay hands on them.

In two ministry trips to Korea, we shared in six different churches, all of which expected us to "knock them down". As my wife likes to share, after hearing our interpreter explain what we were expected to do in our first service, she said to me, "Ben, what are we going to do? We don't have a knock-em-down ministry."

After the message, about two hundred people were lined up in rows across the large auditorium. These people had spent so much time in prayer and worship that they were expecting to feel the power of God when we touched them. Almost without exception, these precious folk reacted like there was a flow of electricity entering their bodies. One by one they went down, some quietly, and others shaking rather violently.

Falling under the power of God is certainly a wonder, because it makes us wonder what is happening, but if it is also a sign, then it should carry a message to us. I believe it certainly does.

Standing is a position of strength. Paul told us to stand firm in our spiritual battles, with all of our armor on (Ephesians 6:13,14). When we stand, we are in a position to defend ourselves and to maintain our self-sufficiency. When we are knocked down by some external power, we become vulnerable and defenseless. I believe that in harmony with many Scripture passages, God chooses to make us sense our weakness, if we are willing, so He can show us His strength.

Falling under the power is a sign that God wants us to know and understand our own helplessness and our dependency on Him. Paul talked about being strong when he was weak. Jesus told him, "My strength is made perfect in weakness." (II Corinthians 12:9)

I believe that falling under the power is a prophetic sign that God is revealing to His church how weak we are without His power. Meanwhile, as we recognize our own weakness, He is going to infuse us with His supernatural power.

Being under the power of God for many is like being under anesthetic, where God is the surgeon, taking out various cancers in our lives. I do believe that we are in a season of deliverance from sins of the flesh and bondages to demonic powers. But for God to do this work, He must first humble us so we will acknowledge our need.

Laughter and Intercessory Weeping

During the nineties a spontaneous explosion of hilarious laughter occurred in many places. These happened in movements such as the Faith Movement, the Vineyard and the Assembly of God. People who were normally respectable and "all together" would burst into uncontrolled laughter and sometimes fall to the floor, laughing hysterically. Even ministers would find themselves unable to preach when hit by laughter. This experience seemed to be more contagious than any known disease, and spread quickly around the world.

At the same time as laughter was breaking out in the church, many people were experiencing a great wave of intercessory anointing. These people might find themselves praying for hours, accompanied by many tears.

I do firmly believe that God is saying something to His church through these signs. First of all, these signs are to unleash the power of our God-given emotions and passions. For too long our flavor of Christianity has been dominated by "left-brained" theologians, who have not had the ability to greatly impact those who are more "right-brained" or emotionally motivated.

During the nineties, I was impressed with the passage in Ecclesiastes 3:4, which tells us that there is a time to laugh and a time to cry. Paul declared in Romans 12:15 that we should rejoice with those who rejoice and weep with those who weep. Psalm 126:5 speaks of sowing in tears and reaping in joy. God is an emotional God, who laughs and weeps, and most of God's great leaders were emotional as well, including Moses, David, Peter and Jesus.

I believe that we will see more healings and conversions as Christians release their emotions to be used by God. I also believe that the release of laughter in the church was a symbol of emotional healing coming to the church. The Bible says that a merry heart does good like a medicine. The laughter that hit the church released many people in their emotions and brought about some real inner healing. God saw His people in great need of deep emotional healing and prescribed laughter.

Shaking

One of the strangest phenomena to observe but probably the easiest to interpret is what we call shaking. Many people who have been what is commonly known as "in the river" have found parts of their body reacting with jerks and shaking out of their physical control. Some of these movements can be quite strong.

When the shaking takes place it may make the person look very undignified and possibly physically retarded. It is a humbling experience, to say the least, and that is something it has in common with all of the previously mentioned signs and wonders. God does not seem to respect our personal pride and dignity when it comes to these unusual experiences.

But what is the message of the shaking sign? This should be a no-brainer. The Bible clearly declares that God will once more shake the earth, and that every thing that can be shaken will be shaken, so that only that which cannot be shaken will remain.

During these days of preparation for the coming of the Bridegroom, God is working on the church. He is not just doing a cosmetic job, but rather He is doing a total remodeling job, starting with the foundation. But to do the job right He first has to separate the good material from the bad. The shaking that has already taken place in the church will continue until only the pure and strong materials will remain. All that is not totally of God will be shaken loose and cast off.

Neither my wife nor myself are very physically sensitive to the presence of God in regards to these manifestations. We have both spent time on the floor, but most of the time, we could have stayed on our feet if we had tried. Both of us have participated to a limited degree in the laughter experience, but it was a rather temporary thing, confined to a few occasions when others were manifesting in a similar fashion.

Until recently, neither of us had been touched by the shaking phenomenon. But while in Korea, I began to feel something happening occasionally while we prayed for people. Like a reaction to a small electric shock, without any feeling of pain, my body would jerk slightly when I felt a stronger than usual anointing. Since that time it has happened on numerous occasions, often catching me off-guard. But it is always reassuring now when it happens, because I am made aware of His presence, and I am reminded that it's not by might, nor by power, but by God's Spirit, that anything will be accomplished.

Gold Appears in Various Places

A very common report in recent years has been that gold has appeared as dust on worshippers and as fillings or crowns in their mouths. I personally have seen a few gold teeth and a few flecks of what appeared to be gold dust on the clothing of people. Others with whom we have talked have witnessed much more than we have, but the sheer volume of reports from various places lends credibility to the phenomenon.

What is the "message of the sign" of the appearance of gold? This is somewhat more difficult for me to interpret than the other signs. But clearly gold has always been a symbol of wealth and prosperity. The appearance of gold would be a sign that God is releasing His wealth on His children.

The wealth that many of us desire is not so much the financial wealth, but the wealth of spiritual possessions such as the fruit and gifts of the Holy Spirit. The greatest wealth comes in friendship, and the greatest friendship we could have is friendship with God. But material or financial prosperity could certainly be included in the application of this truth.

What about the gold teeth, fillings and crowns? The first reason for these would be that people need them and often don't have the finances to pay for them. But as far as the significance of them as signs is concerned, there could be several applications.

The teeth are for breaking up food so that the digestive juices can work quickly on it. They are vital in the process of providing nutrition to the body. Poor teeth would hinder good health. Providing good teeth would symbolize the fact that God is releasing greater revelation in the body of Jesus and He wants us to be able to properly digest the "meat" He wants to give us.

Why then gold, and not just natural tooth material? Possibly for two reasons. First of all, many people wouldn't notice or be able to distinguish the miraculous filling from the rest of the teeth, and God would not receive the glory. Secondly, God wants us to know that He is giving us more than we started with.

God is still speaking that the "Glory of the latter house will be greater than the glory of the former house." (Haggai 2:9) God is combining the concept of the need to be prepared for greater revelation with the fact that He is coming with the riches of His own glory, which will accompany the revelation.

Another possible message of the sign of "gold in the mouth" is the fact that the words we speak are formed by our mouths, and God wants our words to be an expression of the glory of God. Solomon declares:

"A word fitly spoken is like apples of gold in settings of silver. Like an earring of gold and an ornament of fine gold is a wise reprover to an obedient ear." (Proverbs 25:11,12)

Thus, we see a Scriptural comparison of the words we speak and the concept of wealth and beauty, which gold always represents. This may not be the best explanation of the "gold teeth" sign, but it is worthy of consideration of at least one "message of the sign".

Since writing the above comments, this author has heard new and fresh testimony from a close friend and minister who just returned from South Africa and saw many miracles of gold in the mouth and in other places. Other substances like diamonds appeared and vanished when rubbed.

I also read that in the Argentina revival in the past decade, there were so many gold fillings and crowns, etc., that they would only allow those who had received four or more gold fillings to give public testimony, because of lack of time.[9]

VALUE OF MODERN SIGNS

Many people in our contemporary world have reported various signs and wonders in various places. These range from the believable to the bazaar, but many people have found great encouragement, strength and direction from those which they have experienced.

When seeking wisdom or confirmation for making significant decisions, many Christians have been blessed by a divine coincidence, or a wet fleece, or some other apparently miraculous communication from God. These folk often give great glory to God and also use these signs as a powerful witnessing tool. When we can demonstrate that Jesus is still alive and helping us with our situations in life, it gives hope to others that He could do the same for them if they accept Him as Lord and Savior.

As we have clearly shown the witnessing power of signs and wonders is the main reason for God to reveal them and it should be the main reason we seek after them. The incredible evangelistic impact of the miraculous power of God, revealed in the meetings of Reinhart Bonnke in Africa, is the greatest contemporary example of using signs and wonders for the purpose of winning the lost, just like the apostles did in days gone by.

What about the teaching that signs and wonders are useful to get something started, especially on the mission field to get people saved, but we were not intended to live by the miraculous. Rather, we are to live by the principles of wisdom, where we don't need the power of the miraculous nearly as much to bail us out of our problems. Most of our problems are caused by lack of wisdom and discipline in our own lives. Therefore, if we teach self-discipline and good character people won't need God's supernatural help and He won't have to constantly come to our rescue.

This is an argument which has some merit, but leaves out some very important points about the purpose and power of the miraculous.

First of all, it seems clear from biblical and church history that more of the miraculous occurs when new frontiers are being established. My mentor, Elmer Burnette, started at least seven churches. Each one was started through the power of the miraculous. People would come to receive healing and would then get saved. After a time, he would turn the church over to another pastor, who would shepherd the flock in the ways of God, but there would be an ebb in the flow of the supernatural.

Part of the reason for this phenomenon may be that after a church is established, it loses some of its zeal for evangelism and becomes inward focused, instead of outward focused. **As long as there are still people around us who have not had the gospel preached to them with signs following the preaching of the word, we should still be seeking for signs and wonders to bring them to faith in Jesus.**

Another weakness of the theory we are discussing presupposes that God gets tired of us coming to Him to bail us out. God is more concerned about us becoming self-centered and self-sufficient than He is about us coming to Him too often.

It is true that God wants us to avoid the pain and sickness and poverty that results from our lack of self-discipline, because He loves us, but He never gets tired of us coming to Him. The biblical evidence is over-whelming that God wants us to come to Him constantly, and share our hearts with Him. It gives Him the opportunity to have the fellowship with us that He created us for. It also gives Him the opportunity to share His burdens with us.

Consider the beautiful and well-known passage in Matthew 11:28-30. Here Jesus invites all those who are weary or fatigued to come to Him for a break or pause in their labor. He reveals that if they do come to Him and exchange their burden for His yoke, they will get to know Him, and their soul will find a place of rest and refreshment in Him. God never expresses impatience with people who come too many times for help, but He does offer a better way to those who suffer because of their own lack of wisdom.

Another purpose of signs and wonders is for the encouragement or building up of the body of Jesus on the earth. It's not just the non-Christian who needs his faith stimulated; many Christians, if not all, go through times of discouragement and doubt. God does not look on them with disdain, but rather is looking for a vessel who believes God's Word and will exercise faith for a demonstration of God's love and power on their behalf.

Sometimes it is an individual that God will show His power to and sometimes He will do it for a local church or the churches of a city or region or nation. But we know that He does care about His church, just like He cared for the nation of Israel and showed them signs and wonders when they were discouraged. He just needed a Moses or an Elijah or Elisha who had the faith to believe for the power of God to be released. May God raise up many contemporary prophets with a boldness to believe for the power of the supernatural to encourage His people today.

CHAPTER 16

Using God's Complete Arsenal to Facilitate Faith

In this concluding chapter, we want to get very practical and put all this research to good and proper use. It's not enough to know that doing miracles can be a big help in bringing people to faith in God. Nor is it enough to know that kindness and love and/or a quality presentation of the gospel with excellence and creativity will help many people find Jesus. We must be able to actually do these things.

As we have seen God's evangelistic arsenal includes a lot of different weapons. Some of these require a dedication and commitment to study and work hard to develop excellence. Others depend more completely on the ability to draw from the supernatural power of the Holy Spirit. This requires a different type of dedication and commitment, but like the other, it doesn't just fall into our lap. To use any of God's weapons, we must be taught and trained, and we will always pay some price for an effective ministry.

Our Goal

Let's be clear as to what our goal is. Stated simply, this is it:

1. **We want to present the Gospel in a spirit of excellence and integrity with as much grace and love as we possibly can, and ...**

2. We want to back up the Word of the Gospel with a demonstration of the Power of God.

If we develop both of these aspects of our evangelistic arsenal, we will have the biblical **double-barreled shotgun approach** and we will have a much better chance of hitting the target and accomplishing our goal of producing faith in others. This has been God's preferred method over the millennia and it is still His preferred method today. As He did it with Moses, with Elijah, with Peter and Paul, He is still doing it with men and women of God today.

They preached the Word, and God did the signs to confirm the Word. The result was that the people believed God and the people worshipped God, as we discovered many chapters ago. In the remainder of this chapter, we will list two key steps to bring this about today.

I. Preach and Practice the Three E's

The three E's are **Enthusiasm, Excellence and Empathy**. These are the qualities so clearly displayed in some of the most successful evangelical churches that we have researched in this study. Let's take a brief look at each of these.

Enthusiasm: Your genuine enthusiasm says that you are really excited about what you are saying and that you really believe it. If you demonstrate that you are totally sold on what you are talking about, the listener is more inclined to be convinced that what you have will bless them too.

The word "enthusiasm" is from the Greek phrase, "in God". **To be in God is to be enthusiastic.** The Bible says that we are "in Him" in many places, including several times in Ephesians 1.

If the gospel is presented without enthusiasm, we are not representing the gospel well. It is such good news that if we are not excited about it, our listeners will have a hard time believing that it is as good as we claim. If it is that great a gospel, why aren't we showing more emotion and enthusiasm?

Enthusiasm is expressed by the inflection and tone of our voice, and by many other aspects of "body language". We should never treat the gospel as just a part of our system of beliefs. It should always spark fresh excitement in us to think of how much the Father loved us to send His only begotten Son to restore His relationship with us.

That excitement should show in the way we speak, both to Christians and to unbelievers alike. If we have been treating the gospel without the enthusiasm it deserves, we need to confess that sin to God and ask the Holy Spirit to give us a fresh vision of the cross and resurrection.

Excellence: We have the most important mission on earth, and the most costly commodity to dispense to humanity. Should we handle such a valuable gift from God with carelessness and sloppiness? Of course, the answer is no. God's Word and His Good News deserve reverence, respect and excellence in the way we handle it.

Excellence can be applied in many areas of our Christian witness and lifestyle. Our church services should reveal the fact that we care about everything that we do as His representatives.

Without putting excessive focus on external things (at the expense of the issues of the heart), we should do our best to provide an atmosphere of an orderly and happy home, where people feel comfortable and welcome. Of course, we want more than anything else to make God feel welcome in His own house, but we also want people to desire God's house to become their own house as well.

Of course this involves the appearance of the building, both inside and out. I know the struggles of the pastors of small churches with limited finances on this issue, but we too easily get used to things that need repairing or improving. We don't see things through the eyes of a visitor who comes once and sees too many things that are not so excellent. He concludes that this church or pastor doesn't value excellence and that if he really wants to find quality in a church, he will have to look somewhere else. Even great worship and a great message and friendly people will make it difficult for him to want to come back in many cases, especially if he is leadership quality.

Of course, we should, as David did, seek to have excellence in our worship, both in the spirit of our musicians and in their musical giftings. We should also be prepared to honor God and the people's time, by being well-prepared and focused on the issues that the Holy Spirit has led us to focus on. When the Holy Spirit wants to surprise us with something special, the people will usually respond favorably, but if we fail to prepare, we should not use the common expression, "We're just going to let the Holy Spirit lead the service."

Now that we travel in ministry full-time, I have some favorite teachings and messages that I frequently use, and thus I don't always need to do the academic research, etc., that a pastor might do on a weekly basis. Even so, my preparation usually amounts to as much prayer and study as I can find time for, without necessarily knowing what I will be sharing in the service.

For me preparation is not knowing every word that I will share, but rather knowing that I am in touch with the Living Word and His Holy Spirit. Often my decision comes during worship, just before I speak, and often I receive fresh revelation, either during worship or during the message itself. I believe that many of our best results have come when I didn't know what I was going to be speaking before the worship time.

Even with that honest confession, I must say that I am only doing the preaching. I am not leading worship or decorating the sanctuary or giving announcements, etc. I depend on the local people to take care of those details, and I appreciate it when they have shown a love of excellence, both in the spiritual and the natural. What they are actually doing is taking the natural into the realm of the spiritual, so that nothing they do is considered natural, but for them, it is all a spiritual service to God.

Another area in which excellence is commanded by God is in the practice of building up, or edifying each member of the body of Jesus. Notice what Paul tells the Corinthians:

"Even so you, since you are zealous for spiritual gifts, let it be for the edification of the church that you seek to excel." (I Corinthians 14:12)

The word "excel" is the root of excellence and is of course, the verb form. To excel at edifying the church, means to be the best builder that you can be. This is something which needs to be emphasized in our churches. Discouragement is rampant, but if we would all pursue excellence in building up and encouraging one another, discouragement would lose it power to paralyze so many members of the body of Jesus.

The context of the above scripture is the discussion of the purpose of the gift of prophecy. It includes a discussion of why prophecy is more useful than speaking in tongues at the church level. It also includes a couple of strong exhortations to strongly desire to prophesy, because that is one great way to build, or edify the body of Jesus.

Another important aspect of excellence involves taking time to allow **creativity** to flourish. The pursuit of excellence almost always involves the desire to present things in a new and fresh way. Often this can be done through the various arts available to us. Music and drama are powerful tools to present the gospel. Even dance and mime can be a beautiful and successful means of sharing the awesome news of the gospel. We must never let the message become stagnant for believers or unbelievers. Using the power of creativity, we can more easily keep up the flow of enthusiasm, our first "E".

Empathy: This word means the ability to feel someone else's pain or joy, and is a first cousin of the words, love and compassion. If we want to reach people with the gospel in such a way that they will embrace our faith as their own, we must convince them that God has given us a genuine love for them along with an ability to understand them.

My own wife, Brenda, is such a fine example of this important commodity. Her ability to weep with those who weep and feel their pain is something I have never been able to duplicate, except under a strong anointing of the Holy Spirit. For me it is a special happening, but for her it is very natural. But at the same time it is always a supernatural event, when the love of God flows through us.

There are people who will respond to the gospel, based on this kind of love alone. We have seen the response in a number of people who knew that someone was reaching into their hearts with a love-power that they had never known before. Their hearts were conquered and they surrendered to the God who Himself is love.

II. Passionately Pursue the Power of Power

Since the power of signs and wonders cannot be gained by any natural means, we need some special guidelines for developing the second barrel or our "Soul-Winning Shotgun". We will list what we believe are some of the most important points for releasing this power.

A. Earnestly Desire a Revelation of God's Power

To hunger and thirst after righteousness implicitly means that we hunger and thirst for the manifestation of the power of God. For God's righteousness or justice to happen on the earth, miracles must take place. God's justice causes one who has suffered for eighteen years all bent over to be released from a spirit of infirmity on the Sabbath day (Luke 13:16). His righteousness or justice demands that wrongs be made right and that usually requires some supernatural intervention.

We are told to desire spiritual gifts and we know that the apostles cried out for more signs and wonders to give them boldness. Paul fully preached the gospel by adding mighty signs and wonders to the words he preached.

My personal testimony involves confessing my lack of passion or burden as a nineteen-year old Bible College freshman. The result was a powerful desire to see the power of God released on the earth. That passion has been a driving force in my life. It has also been rewarded many times, especially in our overseas ministries.

If you lack the desire for the power of God try reading through the book of Acts every two days, as I did in Bible College. I knew God hadn't changed, but the church certainly had. I cried out for God to wake up His church, which is the greatest sleeping giant on earth. I cried out for revival day after day, shedding many tears in an unusual intercession that would last one or two hours every morning as I read about the early church.

Although I deeply appreciate churches that are passionately committed to winning souls through other methods, my own heart cries out for the "double barrel" ministry of the Word plus Signs following. And, of course, I desire that every skeptical soul has the extra opportunity to believe, because of a demonstration of the power of a supernatural God.

B. Understand the Power Potential of Unity

To better understand my heart on this subject, I highly recommend my first book, *Heal Your Body, Lord*. In this book I reveal the secret power that the various levels of unity can produce. Unity begins with a united heart. David prayed for this in Psalm 86:11.

We can have many conflicting desires, but we need one desire that is so much more powerful than the other desires that it dominates and redirects them, until the desires of our hearts are in total unity.

Some have stated, "We tried unity in our town, but it didn't work." The unity attempted was only a superficial unity, and could not accomplish God's purpose.

Jesus made it clear in His prayer in John 17, that when the disciples would be in unity, the world would believe. My personal conviction is that the world would believe in Him because their unity would release His awesome supernatural power.

Consider these facts:

1. Jesus prayed five times in John 17 for unity.

2. Luke records five times in Acts 1-5 that the church was in "one accord".

3. During this period of unity, the greatest results were recorded. Everyone was healed and thousands were saved.

When divisions began to proliferate, starting in Acts 6, some of the power was lost. At least three cases of sickness, including Timothy's "frequent infirmities", were not immediately healed, according to the epistles of Paul.

I have often publicly stated the following: "If we don't have a passion for unity, we don't know the heart of the Father." A lack of unity is a lack of power, like a car with some of its important parts disconnected from the rest of the vehicle.

But the good news is that we don't have to wait for total unity before we see the faith-building power of signs and wonders. We can work on unity on every level, through the power of prayer, humility and love, at the same time as we witness and cry out to God for the confirmation power of His signs and wonders.

The exciting promise from God that I love so much is found in II Chronicles 16:9:

"For the eyes of the Lord run to and fro throughout the whole earth, to show Himself strong on behalf of those whose heart is loyal to Him."

The word "loyal" in this NKJV translation is also translated, perfect or complete. It could also be translated with the word "united". God is looking for hearts that are totally united or completely loyal to Him. What he promises is that He will show us His power if our hearts or our desires are in unity with His heart.

To me a loyal heart is a heart that agrees with His heart. His heart greatly desires unity and harmony among His children. If we strongly desire unity, we will catch the attention of His heart-searching eyes, and He promises to show His power to us. That means that He will do some great miracles for us. These, of course, can be used to prove to seekers around us that God is real and alive and full of love.

Before leaving this point, I want to re-emphasize the role of humility in producing unity. As Proverbs 13:10 declares, "Only by pride comes contention". It's not so much our doctrines that divide us, but it's our pride in those doctrines. The human ego always wants to be right and look wiser or more righteous than others. Therefore, it becomes very difficult to listen to others, who don't agree with us and to do it with an open mind. I love to debate and prove the other person wrong, but this is my flesh and I must subdue it and replace it with an open heart and mind to listen to others. This is the only way that I can encourage unity with my brothers and sisters.

The Bible promises that God gives grace to the humble, and God's power is released through His gifts of grace. The word Charismatic has the word "Charis" as its root. Charis means grace.

Thus humility releases God's grace, and God's grace releases spiritual gifts, which release God's supernatural power to produce the signs and wonders. For instance, the gifts of healings and miracles, mentioned in I Corinthians 12, are the means of producing many different signs and wonders. These are gifts of grace, which are released and increased through humility.

Now we can see two parallel Biblical laws:

1. Humility produces unity.

2. Unity produces power.

3. Humility releases grace.

4. Grace releases spiritual gifts for signs and wonders.

Thus we see that the source for power always goes back to humility.

C. Be Aggressive and Bold and Go For It

At the same time as we are crying out to God with a passion for the supernatural, and at the same time as we are asking God to unite His church and heal His body, we need to begin to step out in faith and go after the supernatural manifestations of God. Again, our motive is not to prove our spirituality, but rather to bring confirmation to the seekers among us that God is truly with us and able to touch their lives in a very positive way.

There are several things that we can do to get going in a supernatural ministry, besides praying earnestly for the anointing of the Holy Spirit. We will look at what I would consider to be the most important.

1. Study

The first thing I would suggest both to individuals and to churches and church leaders, is to do an intensive study of spiritual gifts. Study all the lists of gifts with a special focus on the context of these gifts. Each of these lists has specific instructions for us before and after the gifts are named. These have been largely ignored when spiritual gifts are taught, and the result has been tragic.

It is very interesting that the Bible does not give us clear definitions or explanations of how these gifts work, but it gives us many instructions about the attitude and purpose of all the gifts. In these instructions we read that each of us is gifted by God, and that the gifts give us our function as members of the body of Jesus. We learn that we ought to see ourselves soberly, knowing that all God's children are important and have an important place in the body of Jesus.

What we do have in Scripture that will help us is a great number of illustrations of spiritual gifts in operation that we can study. For instance, we see Jesus and the apostles releasing the gift of knowledge. Peter knew that Ananias and Sapphira were lying through this gift. Jesus knew what the Pharisees were thinking through this gift.

Peter and John exercised the gift of faith and the gift of miracles when the lame man was healed in Acts 3. There were many examples of the gift of discerning of spirits. Peter told Simon the sorcerer that he perceived that he was bound in iniquity." (Acts 8:23)

Besides doing our own personal study, we also ought to study what others have written from their own research and experience. These can often make the gifts more understandable in a contemporary setting. We will also find that there are different approaches and understandings of the gifts and we can usually learn something new from everyone we study. We don't have to agree with it all, but we can always "eat the meat and spit out the bones."

2. Discover Your Own Gifts

As we study the gifts and ministries in Scripture and in the teachings of others, we may begin to identify with some of them more than others. We may recognize that we have had a strong attraction to certain types of ministry, and that we have already experienced supernatural knowledge or wisdom or discerning of spirits. We may already have seen people healed when we prayed, or we may have spoken special words of encouragement that were in a higher realm than our natural thoughts.

These are strong clues to help us discover what our spiritual gifts are. It is also extremely helpful to receive prophetic ministry from those gifted in confirming these ministries and gifts in the life of an eager believer.

In the past couple of decades, personal prophetic ministry has flourished and matured so that if a person desires confirmation from prophetic ministry, he or she can usually find it. One of the most experienced in this field is Bishop Bill Hamon, the founder of Christian International. He and his ministry have trained thousands of Christians to prophesy with a growing grace and maturity. Many others, such as Rick Joyner, the leader of Morningstar Ministries in North Carolina, have also been training thousands of prophetic people, both young and old. These and many others have written great books on prophetic ministry.

We have personally taught hundreds of people in the United States, Canada and South Korea our "School of Prophetic Ministry 101"in the last few years. The result of that class was the writing of our second book, *The Dynamics of Biblical Prophetic Ministry.*

3. Step Out in Faith

It is very important that we don't just wait for God to superimpose His will on us before we begin to use our gifts. Paul told Timothy to stir up the gifts in him (II Timothy 1:6), and also not to neglect the gifts God had given him (I Timothy 4:14).

Peter admonished us that we were to serve one another with these gifts as good stewards of the manifold grace of God (I Peter 4:10). We have been given gifts by God's grace, and if we don't use them to serve one another we are not being good stewards of God's grace. His grace is a very precious commodity and we have been given stewardship of it. We ought to take seriously this responsibility.

When Paul told Timothy to stir up the gift he had been given, he followed with the familiar statement, "For God has not given us the spirit of fear, but of power and of love and a sound mind." The main reason we don't use our gift, even when we know we have one, is fear. We are afraid we will mess up and look stupid. Or we just don't want people to look at us as if we are a little weird.

But we will never get started if we don't step out in faith. This requires boldness and humility at the same time. We need to express our humanity to those we minister to, so they will allow for our inexperience and immaturity, but we need to also declare that God has asked us to be bold for the sake of His Kingdom.

John Wimber, the founder of the Vineyard movement, who passed on a few years ago, used to tell of how God began to talk to him about His supernatural power to heal and do miracles. He was led to teach his church about physical healing in the atonement. Then God asked him to start praying for the sick. The only problem was that nobody was healed.

Again God compelled him to preach on the subject and pray for the sick. Again no one testified of any miracle. He would have been happy for anything like a small headache or sore toe healed, but nothing happened. This went on for some time. He wanted to quit, but God would not let him.

After many weeks of failure, the first healing took place, to his great delight. After that they came at an accelerating pace. Soon a whole movement was born with a strong focus on the miraculous power of God. The term "power evangelism" was soon coined and hundreds of Vineyard churches exist today because of the "power of power" to convince people that God is alive.

The point is that whether you feel called to prophesy, to do miracles or to heal the sick, never allow yourself to give up. What you desire with your whole heart will be given to you if you are delighting yourself in the Lord (Psalm 37:4).

4. Help Others Activate Their Gifts

When we have learned to use our gifts for the glory of God both in the church and outside the church, we should be striving to help others find their practical place in the body of Jesus. Our goal is, of course, not just to make them feel important, but to strengthen the whole body of Jesus, and to put one more skilled and equipped soldier on the front lines in the fight against the enemy of our Heavenly King.

We can help others find their gifts by teaching them and encouraging them to follow in our footsteps. That is, we teach them to pray, cry out, study and pursue their gifts and callings for the glory of God and the enlargement of His Kingdom.

The Kingdom of God is desperate for spiritual fathers, who will nurture and train the young soldiers for the front lines. We must ourselves move as quickly as possible from student to teacher, and from follower to leader. We must do it with grace and humility, knowing that we have nothing that wasn't given to us. In other words, we didn't and never will earn any of God's gifts. That's why they are called gifts.

If we love God's Kingdom, we will want to be good stewards of His gifts to us. We will seek to multiply them by investing our seeds of potential into the lives of as many others as possible. We are just beginning to learn how to do this ourselves, but many others have done a great job of raising up disciples to extend the Kingdom of God.

WRAPPING UP

It's time now to put the wraps on this study. As much material as we have covered, there is still so much more that could be reviewed. But I believe we have made a very strong point or two. I am also convinced that those who read the results of our research and analysis with an honest heart and mind will desire to break down the walls that divide the church and put together the best from both sides of the wall that has divided the Kingdom team.

It's time to unite God's evangelistic team to advance the yardsticks into the enemy's territory. This is God's vision and plan and He is looking for those who will carry the ball and lead the way.

We have established that signs and wonders have a divine purpose and that at least 90% of recorded conversions in Scripture were made following a clear demonstration of the supernatural power of God. We have further demonstrated that many of the most powerful evangelistic ministries today and in recent history have relied on the power of the miraculous to bring seekers to faith in God.

The largest church in the world, with membership of about three-quarter million strong, was built on the belief and frequent demonstration that God not only saves, but also heals. Today's most successful soul-winner relies on the power of miracles to attract crowds by the millions. He has seen over one million recorded conversions in one public meeting. A healing evangelist in North America routinely sees conversions numbering in the thousands in his meetings.

At the same time others have been quite successful, using a variety of other strategies to win the lost. We admire and respect them for doing so well what they have been called to do.

But what if we could put together the best of both worlds? Would we not have an awesome, unbeatable combination? Would we not have the perfect one-two punch? The fact is that many of the greatest and most successful ministries today are using the best from both camps. But what we lack is the unity and cooperation of both camps joining as one and putting all their resources together.

Now, in conclusion, we must return to our original question. Should we seek or should we not seek signs and wonders? The answer is both yes and no.

We should not seek signs and wonders just for the high we get from them. Neither should we be like the Pharisees and pretend that we want to see the power of God displayed.

But yes, we should seek after signs and wonders and cry out for them with intense passion, for the sake of the Kingdom of God. We need the signs and wonders to reveal to the seeker and the skeptic that God is alive and real, and that He still loves His own special creation. Some will believe without the signs and wonders, but we want to reach everyone with the most convincing evidence possible, so that they will be motivated to make their pact with God.

I close now with an insight from the book of Genesis. Abraham's servant was commissioned to find the bride for Isaac. Abraham promised that the angel of the Lord would go before him and prepare the bride. The servant then asked God for a sign to make it clear who the bride should be.

Because of the sign being fulfilled, neither Rebecca nor her family could say no to Abraham's servant. The important point that I would like to make is this. Rebecca had no idea that there was an Isaac waiting for her, but she was being prepared and being influenced by the Spirit or angel of the Lord.

Rebecca had a servant's heart and was willing to go and serve her new husband, but she didn't know yet who it would be. I believe our mission and calling is to be just like the servant of Abraham's. There are many people out there who are called to be the bride of Christ. The Holy Spirit has been preparing them and they are willing and ready to serve their new bridegroom when they find out who He is to be.

Our job is to demonstrate that we represent their true bridegroom. When the servant came and shared the sign from God, he followed up by giving special gifts to the new bride for his master's son. Even so we should impart gifts from God, starting with the gift of salvation, followed by some of the special gifts of the Holy Spirit.

The Heavenly Bridegroom is waiting. Many beautiful and willing virgins don't yet know who He is. They need to hear from His servants who can verify who they are and whom they represent, with clear signs and wonders that leave no doubt in their minds.

We need to know the importance of our calling to bring the bride to the bridegroom. He is depending on us to bring Him His bride. And if we ask Him, He will give us the gifts to bestow on His bride and He will give us the clear signs and wonders to prove to His bride that He is the one she has been prepared for.

Let us in unity, as servants of God the Father, take His special treasures and find a bride for His Son, Jesus. She will come, when she is convinced by the confirming signs and wonders that He is the Only One for her. When we stand before our Master, we won't have returned to Him with empty hands. Rather, we will say, "I have finished my course, I have kept the faith." In response, He will say to us, "Well done thou good and faithful servant."

Post Script

Congratulations to all who have read this book from cover to cover. I trust you will be rewarded greatly for your hunger and your diligence and persistence. If you have been impacted by the concepts of this book, or if you want to take issue with them, please feel free to communicate with us. Be blessed in Jesus' name!

Ben and Brenda Peters
Open Heart Ministries
15648 Bombay Blvd.
S. Beloit, IL 61080
www.ohmint.org
benrpeters@juno.com

End Notes

[1] Quoted from *Against Heresies* 2, 49:2 by Irenaeus, Ronald A. N. Kydd, *Charismatic Gifts in the Early Church*, (Peabody, MA, Hendrickson Publishers Inc. 1984) p. 44

[2] Philip Schaff, *History of the Christian Church – Volume I*, (Grand Rapids, Michigan, Wm. B. Eerdmans Publishing Company, 1910) p. 118

[3] J. Sidlow Baxter, *Divine Healing Through the Centuries* (Grand Rapids Michigan, Zondervan Publishing House, 1979) pp. 100,101

[4] Dr. R. Edward Miller, *Cry for Me Argentina: Revival Begins in City Bell* (Essex, England: Sharon Publications Ltd., 1988), 42, 43, 45

[5] C. Peter Wagner, *Spreading the Fire* (Ventura, CA, Regal, A Division of Gospel Light, 1994), p.156

[6] Ron McIntosh, *The Quest For Revival* (Tulsa, Oklahoma, Harrison House Inc., 1997) pp. 40, 76

[7] Ibid, pp. 35, 36

[8] Randy Clark, *Power, Holiness, and Evangelism* (Shippenburg, PA: Destiny Image Publishers, 1999) p. 58

[9] Randy Clark, *Power, Holiness, and Evangelism* (Shippenburg, PA: Destiny Image Publishers, 1999) p. 54

About the Author

Ben Peters recognized the call of God on his life as a young child. Through his parents' encouragement and practical motivation, he read and memorized much Scripture as a child and ended up in Seminary in Regina, Saskatchewan, Canada. There he met his future bride, Brenda Pinkerton, and earned his B. A. and M. Div. degrees.

Ben and Brenda have five children. All of them are serving God in various capacities, including pastoring, missions, worship and drama. The two youngest, Timothy and Nathan are presently traveling with them in full time ministry.

Ben has had a wide variety of experiences in his 35 years of full-time ministry. He has been used by God in serving other ministries, in planting churches and Christian schools, and in evangelism and missions. He has written two other books previous to this one. His first book, entitled, *Heal Your Body,Lord,* was used as a text at George Fox University. The second book, *The Dynamics of Biblical Prophetic Ministry,* is used as a text for his "School of Prophetic Ministry 101". He has also taught his books as courses for Christian Leadership University, in Spokane, Washington.

The Peters planted a church in Raymond, Washington, in 1983. In 1997 they were called to transition into a full-time traveling ministry. They formed Open Heart Ministries and began to travel wherever God opened doors, going full-time in 1999. Their focus has been on revealing the open heart of God to everyone and in turn opening the hearts of the people to God. Their ministry has activated thousands of saints and introduced many non-Christians to the love of Jesus through teaching and prophetic ministry. They have ministered in several nations and are often used as conference and camp speakers.

Brenda's high-level enthusiasm and her ability to be real and transparent, has made her a very popular ladies' speaker. She also has been blessed with a dynamic prophetic gift. Together Ben and Brenda minister prophetically to thousands every year and preach and teach reformational and apostolic truth to thousands more.

LaVergne, TN USA
09 July 2010
188909LV00002B/4/A